Competing for Choice

Competing for Choice
Developing winning brand strategies

Lars Finskud

Copyright © 2003 Lars Finskud

First published in Great Britain in 2003 by

Vola Press Limited
79 St John Street, London EC1M 4NR
www.volapress.com

The right of Lars Finskud to be identified as the
author of this work has been asserted by him in
accordance with the Copyright, Designs and
Patents Act 1988.

A CIP record for this book is available from the
British Library

ISBN 0 9545328 1 3

Printed and bound in Great Britain by
Asset Graphics, London
www.asset-graphics.com

Contents

Introduction

At a time when businesses are finding it hard to generate strong growth and profits, it is surprising that many otherwise well-managed companies are either sitting on vast under-utilized resources or are massively misallocating money on initiatives that aren't accomplishing their strategic and brand objectives. Why are these businesses getting it wrong?

In this book, we argue that the reason is twofold. First, managers are failing to recognize that their business and their brand are in fact two interdependent parts of a single dynamic system. Second, they are too ready to accept poor and fragmented data as the basis for their decisions. What they should do, we believe, is to analyze the systems of resources that make up their business and establish a holistic fact base that they can use to formulate robust and dynamically informed strategy.

This, however, is likely to require a change in mindset. Let's begin by considering the fact that living creatures, institutions, and businesses share a fundamental attribute: they all compete for choice.

With bright colors, symmetrical patterns, agility, intelligence, and a multitude of other features, animals compete to be chosen by a suitable mate. This is essential for reproduction and for the survival of the species. Similarly, we are all in our own way competing to be chosen at various instances in our daily lives. At the same time, we are also constantly making choices. As Aristotle said, "The origin of action is choice, and that of choice is desire and reasoning."

In business, the number of people choosing any one brand is not abundant. Businesses compete for the choice of customers or consumers – ideally many and valuable ones. Not only that, they also compete for the choice of other key stakeholders, including the best employees, partners, and investors, and they do so by providing value to these stakeholders, thus contributing to society at large.

In this sense, brands are the vehicles that businesses use to compete for choice. The value proposition, image, and values that companies provide and embed in their brands is the basis for earning the choice of customers and stakeholders.

But competing for choice isn't easy. Today's rapidly changing world of geopolitical shifts, industry deregulation, intensifying competition, and empowered consumers means that management must earn and continue to earn the choice of multiple stakeholders under conditions that are highly complex and dynamic.

Despite this, companies frequently make decisions about how to compete for choice on the basis of intuition rather than solid fact. We believe that a deep understanding of the dynamics of business and stakeholder choice can complement intuition and yield unexpected new insights. As such, it will help a company to make better-informed strategic decisions.

The approach described in this book recognizes that every company is unique and faces its own particular set of challenges. It draws on ideas from a number of scientific fields and has been developed through many years of research and practice. It has been tried, tested, and refined through work on a wide range of problems with a variety of brands in a host of different industries.

The insights presented here have helped many companies to rethink their approach to strategy, allocate their investments more effectively, and transform their business performance. I hope this book will encourage many more senior managers, and especially chief executives, to follow in their footsteps and harness the power of competing for choice.

1

Competing
for choice

Main themes

- When asked "What are you competing for?" most managers will answer "Competitive advantage" or "Market share." But neither of these things translates into concrete, actionable measures – things a company can do to improve its performance. The right answer to the question is "Customer choice."

- The opportunities for consumers to make choices between different brands are multiplying rapidly. Yet there is only a finite number of consumers who choose any one brand. These customers thus represent a scarce resource.

- In such an environment, formulating strategy is complex. To get it right, managers must set strategy in the context of competing for consumer and stakeholder choice. Brands play a vital role as the focal point for all these choices.

- When evaluating their business performance, managers must choose their market metrics with great care. Brand awareness is *not* a reliable guide to business performance. Instead, *brand choice* is what drives market share. Conviction – a customer's certain future choice of a brand – is the key brand parameter.

The essence of strategy is choice, so choice must be at the core of strategy development. Business strategy is about making the right choices on how and where to compete for which choice with the aim of achieving profitability and long-term value creation.

In a report on the future of the company, *The Economist* pondered on the environment in which companies operate today:[1]

> That environment is dominated by one thing: choice. Technology and globalization open up ever more opportunities for individuals and firms to collect information and conduct activity outside traditional structures.

> As Robert Reich, a secretary of labor under Bill Clinton, points out, "We are entering the age of the Terrific Deal where choices are almost limitless and it is easy to switch to something better." While the age of mass production lowered the costs of products at the expense of limiting choices – Henry Ford famously said that you could have a car in any color as long as it was black – modern "flexible" production systems usually both lower costs and increase choice.

> Consumers have more choice over where they spend their money. Producers have more choice over which suppliers to use. Potential shareholders have more choice over where to put their money.

What does this imply for strategy in business?

It has long been recognized that robust strategy plays a crucial role in any successful enterprise. Business leaders and academics have produced a vast literature on the subject, with Michael Porter's *Competitive Strategy*[2] widely considered to be the seminal treatment.

Yet despite this, there are two key observations about strategy that hold true:

- It is complex.

- Many still get it wrong.

The reasons for this are manifold. Among the culprits are a failure to articulate business and market structures; a lack of clarity on the interdependences within and between systems and management initiatives over time; a high degree of subjectivity in terms of the implicit assumptions that are made; "fact-free" decision making; and differing objectives among the people involved at various steps in the strategy process.

Often, companies regard strategy as a matter of beating the competition by focusing on becoming good at one or more established processes such as cost reduction, process reengineering, total quality management, or customer relationship management. Although the initiatives may be worth

1 Notes appear at the end of each chapter.

while and the objective of differentiating a company from its competitors is sound enough, what lies behind them is rarely articulated. *What is it that the company is competing for?*

Arguably, this is the most fundamental question for a business to ask. Answer it properly, and you will have a basis for setting out clear strategic priorities and principles. But the answers that most managers give – "Competitive advantage" or "Market share" – don't provide this kind of robust foundation for strategy. After all, competitive advantage has no meaning in itself if a company doesn't fully appreciate what it is competing *for*. As for market share, it is an aggregate metric – a function of several factors.

So what is the right answer? Quite simply: choice. Companies have to compete for customers to choose their brand day in, day out.

Choice is key

"Choice: The act of choosing…preferential determination between things proposed"   *Shorter Oxford English Dictionary*

We believe that business strategy is about how a company makes choices to compete for stakeholders' choices with the aim of achieving profitability. In this process of competing for choice, the brand is the focal point. The aim of this book is to give managers a clear understanding of how stakeholder choice structures work and so enable them to choose the right initiatives to apply in the right places to achieve long-term value creation at their own companies.

Let's start with a basic question: What is it that *any* company is trying to do?[3] In most cases, the answer boils down to convincing your target customers to buy, on a repeated basis, the value proposition (product, services, and intangibles) that your company is offering.

There is no business without choice. Hotels must get guests to walk through the door. Airlines need passengers. Without customers, consumers, or clients, a business can't justify its existence.[4] So, yes, business is about competition, but more precisely, it is about competing for customers' choice in an increasingly competitive world.

However, it is not only customers that choose a company. Choice is also exercised by other stakeholders, including employees, partners, and investors. Ideally, a company will want to be the preferential choice of *all* its valuable stakeholders.

This puts a different spin on the nature of competition between firms. The traditional view of companies competing for market share is inadequate because it doesn't explain what a company actually needs to *do* in order to increase market share.

Phil Knight, CEO of Nike, put it like this: "Basically, when you go to buy a pair of shoes you're not buying one from each company. You're going to buy one pair and we are going to try as hard as we can to make that shoe Nike."[5]

That makes a lot of sense, because when consumers go to buy anything from toothpaste to trainers, few will buy several different brands at the same time. So from a brand perspective there are only a finite number of choices to be made in favor of either your brand or your competitor's. Just as there are a limited number of specialists in a given field, customers loyal to your brand are not abundant. Indeed, for most companies they are a scarce but critical resource. They are scarce because they are difficult to accumulate.

Take a big consumer goods brand. Out of 1,000 people, as many as 950 may be aware of it, but typically only a small fraction of that group will emerge as convinced "choosers" of the brand.

Exhibit 1.1
The two axes of brand value management
The ability to justify a price premium and the number of customers choosing a brand

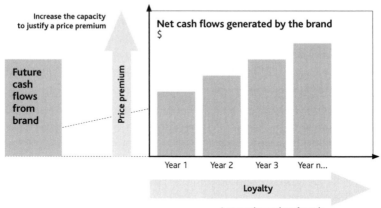

Put simply, tomorrow's cash flows stem from the number of convinced choosers (next-time customers) of a company's brand and the financial contribution that each chooser (customer) brings (number of customers x their purchase frequency x the price they will pay = revenue). The two factors that drive brand cash flow – justifying the price premium and increasing the number of people who choose the brand (and the number of times they choose it) – are illustrated in Exhibit 1.1. A company must find a sustainable balance between the number of choosers of the brand and the price premium charged in order to generate sufficient funds not only to stay in business, but also to provide a return for investors.

Justifying the price premium

The whole area of pricing is complex to say the least, and rare is the company that appreciates the finer aspects of this important management tool. But achieving such an understanding is well worth the effort because any pure price increase (or decrease) goes straight to the bottom line.

Exhibit 1.2
Price premiums and discounts

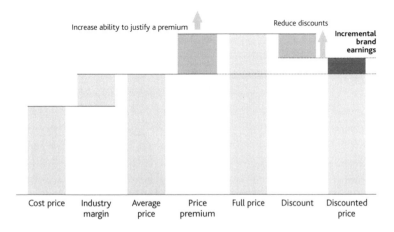

For any brand there are two key levers that affect pricing, as shown in Exhibit 1.2. One is discounting. There is a general tendency on the part of management to rely on discounting and price reduction as the main way to win more choosers and so gain volume. To be sure, price is a potent volume lever in most cases. But managers often squander profit by offering unnecessary discounts – for instance, to already loyal customers who are willing to pay the full price – because they make the mistake of assuming discounting is the *only* driver of volume.

The other lever is justifying the price premium. The mechanics of this aren't always well understood. Few managers pay enough attention to providing a brand proposition with a high degree of "values fit," or match between consumer values and brand values. Yet values fit is one of the main factors determining people's willingness to pay a price premium, and it transcends economic categories. Teenagers don't usually fall into the category of wealthy consumers, but they are often willing to pay a substantial price premium for the brand of trainers that embodies the values to which they aspire. Getting the right values fit will in virtually all cases reduce price elasticity and transform the shape of the volume/price curve. We will return to values fit in chapter 4.

Increasing the number of choosers of the brand

While both axes in Exhibit 1.1 are equally critical to generating top-line revenue, the remainder of this section will focus on the horizontal axis: increasing the number of future "certain choosers." As we have seen, a company's current cash flow derives from those customers who chose (and paid for) its brand yesterday and today. This cash flow may come from a small number of people paying a high premium, or a large number of people paying a low premium.

Exhibit 1.3
Issues in earning customer choice

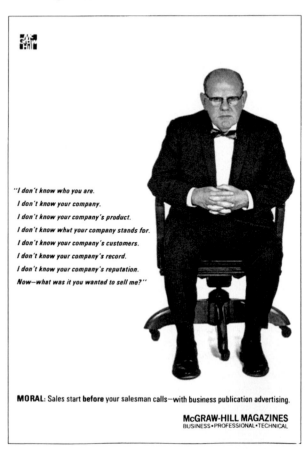

The 1958 "Man in the chair" advertisement from McGraw-Hill demonstrates that the challenges a company needs to overcome in order to earn choice have been recognized for decades (Exhibit 1.3). Unfortunately, that doesn't mean they are always tackled effectively. Below we outline some key insights that will help managers begin to approach these challenges in a more structured way and apply the right management initiatives at the right stages.

The secrets of customer choice

The starting point is to establish a clear view of consumer choice structures based on solid fact. Our extensive brand and market research has generated a number of insights, three of which are particularly important to strategic brand management:

1 There is a quantifiable customer choice chain for every brand.

The chances that a consumer will choose a particular brand range from zero for a brand of which the consumer is totally unaware to near-certainty for a brand that the consumer "swears by" and purchases again and again without fail. If we take a representative sample of 1,000 individuals, it's likely that only a small fraction will be regular and loyal customers of a given brand; the rest will be unaware of it, or aware but uninterested, or inclined to purchase it only occasionally.

This idea of grouping people according to their attitude toward a brand can be represented visually in the form of a "customer choice chain" like the one illustrated in Exhibit 1.4.[6] The size of the boxes reflects the number of people who are at each stage, so the boxes are large at one end (with many people aware of the brand), and small at the other (with relatively few loyal consumers who repeatedly choose the brand). Between these two extremes are a number of intermediate stages through which consumers will pass on their way towards making a purchasing decision in favor of one brand or another. Each stage in the customer choice chain is described in detail in the next chapter.

The customer choice chain structure has been validated through research conducted with hundreds of brands and thousands of consumers, in several countries, across sectors, and over a number of years. It holds true for more than 90 percent of major brands; the exceptions tend to be in the luxury goods and pharmaceutical sectors.

We were intrigued to discover that more than half of all the brands we researched generated more "refusers" – people who will certainly not choose these brands – than convinced choosers. Quite a few of these brands are

Exhibit 1.4
The customer choice chain
The chain is made up of people grouped according to their relationship with the brand

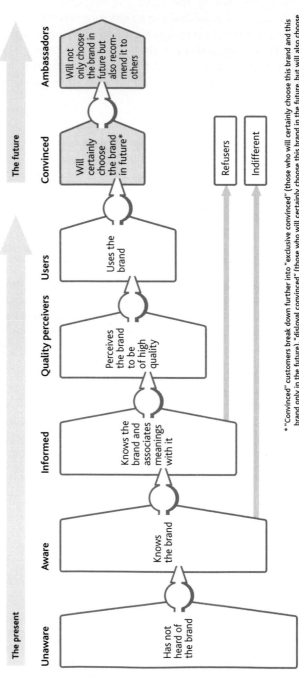

* "Convinced" customers break down further into "exclusive convinced" (those who will certainly choose this brand and this brand only in the future), "disloyal convinced" (those who will certainly choose this brand in the future, but will also choose competing brands), and "virtual convinced" (those who haven't yet used the brand but will certainly do so in the future).

likely to have suboptimal returns on their brand-building investments. Although generating refusers may not be entirely avoidable, managers should take steps to keep the numbers as low as possible to minimize negative word of mouth and to enable investments to be focused on segments with low refusal propensity.

2 Awareness does not correlate with market share.

Though awareness is naturally a prerequisite for conscious choice, research shows that there is no correlation between the number of "aware" consumers and market share. Managers often judge a brand's success by the level of awareness (whether prompted or spontaneous) that it enjoys, but awareness is not a valid measure of either brand or business performance. Far from being an end in itself, awareness is only the first stage in the choice chain.

As Exhibit 1.5 shows, many brands that register high levels of awareness (shown on the horizontal axis on the graph), such as Pepsi-Cola, Fanta, and Skoda, nevertheless score low on the scale of certain future choice, or conviction (vertical axis).

Exhibit 1.5
Awareness versus conviction

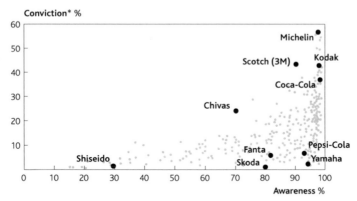

* Certain future choice of the brand ("If I should purchase this type of product I would *definitely choose* this brand")
Source: Megabrand, France, 1994

For another example of high awareness coinciding with low market share, consider the dot-com companies that lavished millions of dollars on advertising campaigns. In most cases, the campaigns generated temporary awareness but failed to produce actual customers because little attention was devoted to understanding how to earn customers' choices. Nor did the companies appreciate the time it takes not only to build awareness but to move people through successive stages from awareness to becoming users and regular choosers of a brand.

Exhibit 1.6
Conviction correlates with market share

A–H: Individual consumer brands within same category

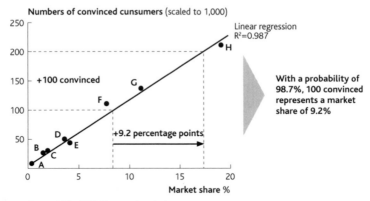

Numbers of convinced cunsumers (scaled to 1,000)

Linear regression
R²=0.987

H

+100 convinced

G

F

+9.2 percentage points

D

B
C
E

A

Market share %

With a probability of
98.7%, 100 convinced
represents a market
share of 9.2%

Source: NRA, 1999; Vanguard analysis

3 Conviction is the key brand metric.

Future cash flows are driven by the number of customers who will choose
and pay for the company's brand proposition tomorrow and into the future
on a continuous basis. These are the "convinced" consumers.[7] Not
surprisingly, our research shows that a strong correlation exists between
convinced users of a brand and its market share (Exhibit 1.6).

Unfortunately, the fact that market share is nothing more nor less than the
manifestation of consumer choice is not yet widely recognized. As a result,
managers talk about market share and competitive advantage without any
clear idea of how to secure consumers' choices in practice. Until they make
an explicit causal link between market share and consumer choice, the
performance of their business will continue to be a black box to them,
and critical questions like those featured in Exhibit 1.7 will go unanswered.

Exhibit 1.7
Opening the black box

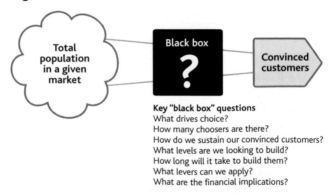

Total
population
in a given
market

Black box

?

Convinced
customers

Key "black box" questions
What drives choice?
How many choosers are there?
How do we sustain our convinced customers?
What levels are we looking to build?
How long will it take to build them?
What levers can we apply?
What are the financial implications?

Exhibit 1.8
A model comparison

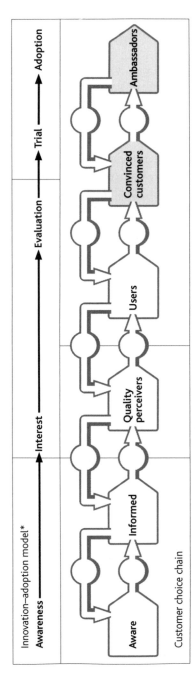

Innovation–adoption model*

Awareness → **Interest** → **Evaluation** → **Trial** → **Adoption**

Aware → Informed → Quality perceivers → Users → Convinced customers → Ambassadors

Customer choice chain

* From Everett M. Rogers, *Diffusion of Innovations*, Free Press, 1962, as cited in Philip Kotler, *Marketing Management*, Prentice Hall, 2003.

Put simply, most managers don't fully understand how to turn potential purchasers of their brand into loyal customers. They lack clarity on how the choice process works and the external factors and management initiatives that influence it.

Why is this so? The main reason, we believe, is the prevailing management focus on tangible assets and resources. Policies and decisions tend to be geared to influencing the numbers that appear in a company's profit and loss account. Few companies have conducted a rigorous analysis of customer choices across segments and markets and over time.

Part of the problem has been the lack of appropriate management tools. Existing customer purchase frameworks don't really fit the bill. Take the "innovation–adoption" model, with its sequence of awareness, interest, evaluation, trial, and adoption (Exhibit 1.8). Though intuitively appealing, it is flawed. For one thing, it fails to distinguish between the stages consumers are at in the choice chain and the levers that can be applied. A simple example of this is "trial," which is a marketing lever (as applied in a sales promotion), and not a state in which people reside.

Although such frameworks have been developed through deductive means and make intuitive sense, they don't provide a sound basis for understanding performance through time. The customer choice chain marks an important step forward in this respect. It allows managers to monitor post-purchase behavior and measure levels of conviction and loyalty among users of a brand. It provides a means of tracking customer flow rates between different stages in the chain, including back-flows. Best of all, it gives managers the means to obtain the solid, up-to-date information and analysis they need to put strategic thinking and decision making on a much firmer footing.

To understand and manage their brand's performance, executives need a robust framework that takes into account the dynamics of customer choice in a changing environment. They also need to establish meaningful and appropriate performance metrics, and monitor them rigorously.

A good starting point is to articulate the customer choice chain and address a few key issues: How many people reside at each point in the choice chain? How do people move along it? And what motivates them to move in either direction?

Notes

1 "The future of the company: A matter of choice," *The Economist*, 22 December 2001, pp. 82–4.

2 Michael E. Porter, *Competitive Strategy: Techniques for analyzing industries and competitors* (Free Press, New York, 1980).

3 Except companies in monopoly situations.

4 We use the terms "customers" and "consumers" interchangeably throughout the book to refer to end users.

5 In *Branded*, BBC2, 15 February 1997.

6 This framework was first identified in 1994 following extensive research in France involving 300 brands, 3,000 consumers, and 78 key brand and population parameters. *See* Patrick Duquesne and Lars Finskud, "Légitimer la prime de marques," *La Revue des Marques*, 1995, Number 9, pp. 31–3.

7 We define "convinced" consumers as people who state that they will certainly choose a given brand next time they make a choice within its category.

2

Uncovering hidden
potential for growth

Main themes

- There is a customer choice chain for every brand. In most businesses focused on consumers, "convinced" customers represent the main source of future cash flows.

- Few companies have articulated and quantified the customer choice chain for their business. As a result, the investments they make in marketing and brand building are not earning good returns.

- Without understanding how potential and actual customers are distributed along the choice chain, managers can't make informed decisions about which levers to apply to improve what aspects of brand performance.

- Effective strategy development and performance measurement both hinge on understanding how many people reside at each stage in the choice chain, and how much they are worth to the company.

- Branding and marketing are two very different things. Branding is about competing for choice. Marketing is one among many levers that can be applied in the process of competing for choice.

- Though any company will want its brand to be chosen by many consumers, usually only a small sub-segment will be genuinely attractive – that is, of high value. Good customer segmentation is indispensable to allow managers to focus on earning the choice of these customers and to avoid generating "refusers."

Many companies neglect to measure intangible resources such as those in the customer choice chain. As a result, they may be underutilizing them to a massive extent. In other words, they are failing to move people effectively along the choice chain to the value-generating stages.

How and why do consumers choose a particular brand? To understand the choices they make, managers must first articulate and quantify the choice process. Armed with this knowledge, they can start to identify the various choice drivers for different segments and work out which lever to apply where to optimize the choice process, so minimizing the number of consumers who stick at early stages in the choice chain.

The customer choice chain, as we saw in chapter 1, identifies the various phases of development in consumers' attitude toward or relationship with a brand. The main stages in the sequence are:

- **Unaware**: people who haven't heard of the brand.

- **Aware**: people who know about the brand.

- **Informed**: people for whom the brand generates evocations or associations.

- **Quality perceivers**: people who perceive the brand as of good quality.

- **Users**: consumers who have used or are using the brand.

- **Convinced**: consumers who will certainly choose the brand next time, but will also choose competing brands.

- **Exclusive convinced**: consumers who will certainly choose the brand next time and will refrain from choosing competing brands.

- **Ambassadors**: consumers who will certainly choose the brand next time and will also actively recommend it to other people, thus generating positive word of mouth.

Once it has been populated with data, the choice chain can be viewed as a snapshot showing how many people reside at each successive stage at a given point in time. Managers can use it to assess their brand's performance and to analyze *why* individuals reside at any one stage in the choice chain and *what it takes* to encourage them to move further along.

Exhibit 2.1 shows a customer choice chain for a European financial services brand. It starts with a total market population of 1,000 people at one end of the chain and ends with 38 "ambassadors" at the other. The drop in numbers from one stage in the chain to the next is shown as a percentage: for instance, 26 percent of all "quality perceivers" fail to become "users" of the brand.

In the large chevron for each stage, we give the *cumulative* number of consumers who either are still residing at that stage or have progressed

Exhibit 2.1
Customer flows along the choice chain
Disguised financial services example

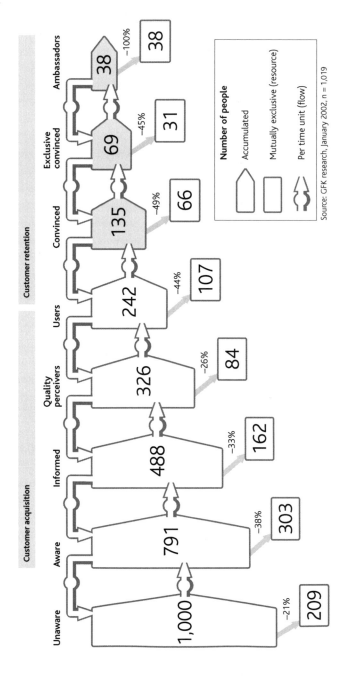

Source: GFK research, January 2002, n = 1,019

beyond it along the choice chain: thus a total of 791 people are "Aware," but many of these have moved on to become informed, quality perceivers, users, and so on. In the small box for each stage, we give the number of people who *actually reside* at that stage in the chain: thus 303 people are "Aware," but not informed, or quality perceivers, or users, and so on. The distinction between these two ways of representing data has important implications for the use of the customer choice chain as a strategic tool; for further explanation, *see* text panel "What are resources?"

Benchmarking performance

Once established, a fact-based choice chain like the one illustrated in Exhibit 2.1 can be analyzed in any number of ways to generate insights and, more important, prompt further questions about performance.

At a basic level, the choice chain can be analyzed in great detail across demographic segments, regions, and so on. In addition, it can be used as a benchmark to measure a brand's performance against competing brands

Exhibit 2.2
Comparing customer choice chains in fast foods
Canada, general population, 1999, scaled to 1,000   Drop-out rates shown in *italics*

	Aware	Informed	Quality perceivers	Users	Convinced	Retention ratio*
Burger King	953	719	493	229	96	10%
	−25%	−31%	−54%	−58%		
Harvey's	886	639	516	237	105	12%
	−28%	−19%	−54%	−56%		
KFC	909	746	472	303	107	12%
	−18%	−37%	−36%	−65%		
McDonald's	985	819	481	456	173	18%
	−17%	−41%	−5%	−62%		
Wendy's	884	662	578	269	142	16%
	−25%	−13%	−53%	−47%		

* "Convinced" as a percentage of "aware"
Source: Print Measurement Bureau, n = 7,473

in its sector, as illustrated in Exhibit 2.2, which reveals, for instance, that McDonald's has the highest retention ratio of the five fast-food companies studied. More important, the choice chain enables managers to monitor brand performance and set objectives and aspirations over time. Although benchmarking is "nice to have" information, it is managers' understanding of the workings of the system and the choice processes within it that yields the most valuable and productive insights.

The customer choice chain of the Canadian fast-food company Harvey's in Exhibit 2.2, for instance, prompts the question: Why does the brand start with a high awareness level – 886 out of a sample of 1,000 people – yet end up with just 105 convinced customers? What are the hurdles preventing people from moving along the choice chain?

Exhibit 2.3
Measuring efffectiveness in achieving customer choice

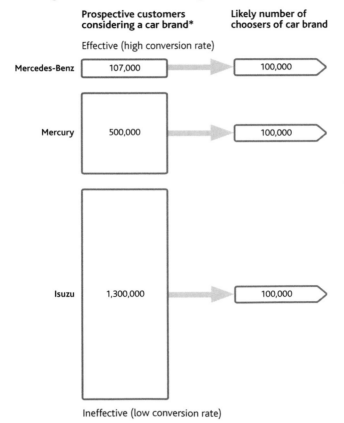

Benchmarking performance

Uncovering hidden potential for growth

* Consideration is defined here as being in the market to buy and having to make a choice between no more than three brands.
Source: CNW Marketing Research, US, 2000; "Revving up auto branding," *The McKinsey Quarterly*, 2002 Number 1.

Harvey's does at least enjoy a high ratio of quality perceivers. If we look at McDonald's, we can see that it suffers from a high drop-out rate between "informed" and "quality perceivers": 41 percent as against 19 percent for Harvey's. However, McDonald's performs much more strongly at the next stage in the chain: once people are quality perceivers, the vast majority (all but 5 percent) move on to become users. As these examples illustrate, benchmarking choice chain performance makes it easy for managers to establish a broad picture of the particular problems and opportunities encountered by their brands.

Sometimes it can be helpful to analyze the customer choice chain the other way around. Imagine a car maker that needs to sell 100,000 units of its new model to be successful. How many potential prospects would it need to persuade to consider its brand in order to achieve this goal? Exhibit 2.3 compares three brands and shows that Mercedes achieves a truly impressive conversion rate, with 93 percent of all US car buyers who considered a Mercedes in 2000 actually buying one. Mercury and Isuzu have to attract far larger numbers of prospects to shift the same number of cars.

Whichever way you look at it – from a given starting point or from a desired outcome – you can use the customer choice chain to assess how effectively a brand converts unaware people into active choosers.

Levels, levers, and influencing factors

Let's now consider how consumers move along the choice chain. Before a company can decide where to apply management levers or make investments to encourage this movement, it will need to understand three important factors:

- The *resource levels*, or number of people residing at each stage.

- The *flow rates*, or rate and speed at which people move from one stage to another. (Here it's important to remember that flows go in *both* directions: just as consumers can progress from "user" to "convinced," for instance, they can move backwards from "convinced" to "user.")

- The *leverage points*, which involve assessing *where* to leverage (to what degree do resources sit under-utilized at early stages in the choice chain?), and *what effect* specific management levers might have (how potent are management levers and other influencing factors in causing people to move between stages?)

What are resources?

A resource is "a stock or supply of money, materials, staff, and other assets that can be drawn on by a person or organization in order to function effectively." *New Oxford Dictionary of English*

In everyday life we encounter resources all the time. The water in a bathtub, the trees in a park, the people in an office, and the money in your pocket are all resources.

A fundamental characteristic of a resource is that its level (or "health") can change only by filling up (accumulating) or draining away (depleting) over time. Thus the level of any resource equals what has ever been gained minus what has ever been lost. The balance of money in a bank account equals all the money ever deposited less all the money ever withdrawn from that account.

The "filling" and "draining" of a resource can only be driven by the in-flows to and out-flows from the resource, measured in flow rates (Exhibit A). A useful way to think about these flow rates is in terms of electric pumps, which pump into and out from the resource at variable speeds.

Exhibit A
Flow rates and resource levels
Stocks or resource levels can be changed only through their in-flows and out-flows

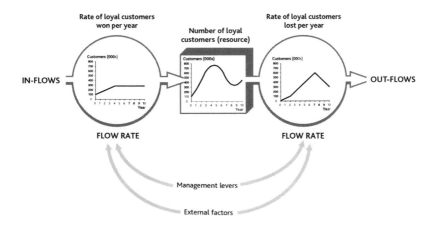

Resources in business

A business is a system of resources. For a company to function requires interactions between many different types of resource. Some are common to most businesses (cash, stock, staff, customers); others are industry-specific (distributors for a drink producer, fuel stations for a petrol company).

A company's resources are a combination of tangible (cash, plant, staff) and intangible (reputation, skills) (Exhibit B). Tangible resources are easy to recognize, count, and measure. Intangible resources are much harder to quantify and more likely to be overlooked, yet they often have a huge impact on company performance. Moreover, they can be just as responsive as tangible resources to management actions such as customer targeting or staff hiring. Indeed, intangible resources are often key to the success or failure of a strategy.

Resources can also be classified according to whether they are under the direct or indirect control of the company. Staff skills are an example of directly controlled resources; customers and reputation are indirectly controlled, but still represent important components in the total system.

Exhibit B
Types of resource

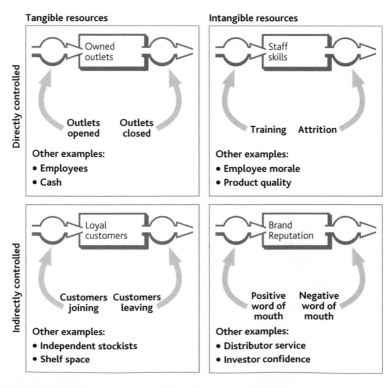

Making better decisions

Seen in this light, a company's set of resources, the way they interact with one another, and the health (or level) of these resources relative to those of competitors define that company's uniqueness and determine its performance. Management's ability to combine, leverage, and grow resources at a faster rate than competitors has a deep influence on the company's long-term success. A prerequisite for any effective strategy is that managers establish clarity on their business's resources, understand their interdependency, and identify the drivers of growth and depletion for each – and then take steps to apply the right management levers, to the right degree, at the right time.

Resource in- and out-flows are influenced directly or indirectly by management initiatives; for instance, customer loyalty programs seek to reduce out-flows from the customer base, while sales efforts tend to be aimed at increasing in-flows of customers. In other words, management initiatives affect the speed at which the electric pumps are running.

It follows that a company should be interested in monitoring not only its current level of customers but also the *rate* at which it is winning and losing customers. What appears on the surface to be a low customer loss rate may in fact disguise a very high churn. For instance, a loss rate of two customers per month may be the net result of eight customers won and ten lost – a very different picture that could have important strategic implications.

Moreover, analyzing the *actual* customers won and lost often yields intriguing insights. Customers won might have lower average volume consumption than customers lost, or use a greater number of competing products. Either would be an essential piece of information to help managers understand current performance and respond appropriately.

Depending on what managers are trying to analyze and understand, resources can be aggregated or disaggregated. For instance, customers can be categorized by geographical area, or according to consumption profile, or both. The degree of aggregation or detail with which resources are described in the business system must be driven by management's ability both to distinguish their drivers of growth and to identify levers that can be applied specifically to them.

The "customer choice chain" groups potential and actual customers into a series of resource stages that are defined by the relationship these customers have with the brand in question. As Exhibit C illustrates, there are two ways of looking at the customer choice chain. What distinguishes the resource-based view from the research-based view is that the categories are mutually exclusive: one person can reside at only one resource stage.

Exhibit C
Two views of the customer choice chain

Scaled to 1,000

 Flow rate

Research-based view

(Cumulative populations; one person may be represented in several boxes)

Total	Aware	Informed	Quality perceivers	Users	Convinced	Ambassadors
1,000	791	488	326	242	135	38
	(includes informed, quality perceivers, users, convinced, and ambassadors)	(includes quality perceivers, users, convinced, and ambassadors)	(includes users, convinced, and ambassadors)	(includes convinced, and ambassadors)	(includes ambassadors)	

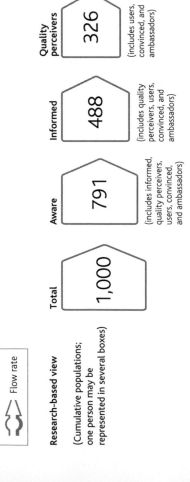
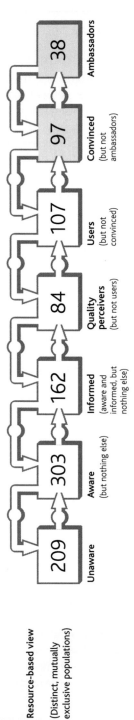

Resource-based view

(Distinct, mutually exclusive populations)

Unaware	Aware (but nothing else)	Informed (aware and informed, but nothing else)	Quality perceivers (but not users)	Users (but not convinced)	Convinced (but not ambassadors)	Ambassadors
209	303	162	84	107	97	38

However, a consumer on the right-hand side of the chain will typically have progressed through the earlier stages over a period of time: for instance, a "convinced" consumer will most likely have started out unaware, become aware, then informed, then a quality perceiver, then a user, and then convinced. How long a consumer spends at any stage depends on the individual; some may move rapidly along the chain, while others may stay at a given stage (quality perceiver, say) for years. The people residing at the different resource stages represent different levels of real or potential value for the brand.

Using the choice chain helps companies to understand consumers' residency at each of the resource stages. In terms of branding, the customer choice chain will reveal which resources are under-utilized or ignored in the current strategy; for instance, a brand may have a large group of quality perceivers who don't move up to become users.

Finally, the choice chain helps companies understand that it takes different kinds of effort and investment to influence the various flow rates to move consumers along the choice chain from one stage to the next. The result: a better use of investments and a more effective marketing spend.

Most organizations have poor information on their "stocks" of customers, and in particular on the rate at which these customers are moving from stage to stage. Establishing resource-based intelligence will give them a much sounder basis from which to formulate strategy and make important decisions about their brands.

The number of people currently residing at any of the stages in the choice chain is not random. A multitude of factors influence people to move in either direction along the chain. The current level at any stage is always the result of the rate at which it has built up or depleted over time. For example, a brand that has won ten new customers per week and lost five per week over a period of ten weeks will see a net gain of 50 customers.

What are the implications of this in terms of strategy? At present, most companies use the details of their past performance to predict and plan what their future performance might be. This approach might just about work in a world where nothing much changes from one year to the next – but life isn't like that. You simply can't use past performance as a predictor of future performance.

A much better approach, in our view, is to stop looking through the rear-view mirror and direct investments and management efforts at the factors that drive heavy flows of people along the customer choice chain. To do that, we need to identify what these factors are and analyze them with a high degree of rigor. So we now go on to consider each stage in the choice chain in more detail.

From unaware to aware

The first transition in the customer choice chain is from unaware to aware. Making a potential customer aware of your brand is usually a prerequisite for moving that customer further along the choice chain. Awareness is often driven by advertising, but can sometimes be created by other factors such as word of mouth or intensity of presence (Exhibit 2.4).

In brand management, the starting point is to define the total potential market for a brand's value proposition. This can range from a major part of the population (for a utility company, say) to a narrow group of people for whom the proposition might be relevant. For a fashion brand such as Hennes & Mauritz, for instance, the target is trendy teenagers and young people; at the other end of the spectrum, Saga targets people over 50 for its magazine, holidays, and financial services. Age is a fairly crude basis for segmentation, but building in other parameters such as values and needs can help develop a more potent, rounded, and nuanced profile of potentially relevant segments.

Even at this early stage in the chain, the ability to identify appropriate segments within the wider population is crucial. Though this segmentation is not meaningful in itself, since awareness does not correlate with choice,

Exhibit 2.4
The transition from unaware to aware

Examples of external factors and management levers

External factors (indirect control)

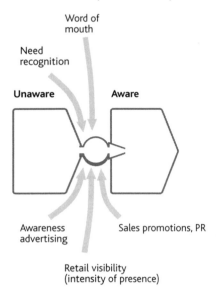

Word of mouth

Need recognition

Unaware   **Aware**

Awareness advertising   Sales promotions, PR

Retail visibility
(intensity of presence)

Management levers (direct control)

it does enable managers to focus their efforts on moving the relevant individuals, as opposed to anyone and everyone, further along the chain.

From aware to informed

Once potential customers are aware of the brand, the next step is to make them informed about the brand proposition (Exhibit 2.5). By "informed," we mean that that the brand evokes various associations that act as a mental model of what it is about. For instance, the Evian brand may be associated with water, purity, the Alps, minerals, and France.

In the context of the choice chain, our concern at this stage is not so much the precise nature of these associations – what might be positive to people some can be negative to others – but rather the brand's ability to generate a rich set of associations among potential customers.

Needless to say, those with positive associations typically move on to become choosers of the brand, while those for whom the brand conjures up negative connotations may well become refusers.

Exhibit 2.5
The transition from aware to informed

Examples of external factors and management levers

External factors (indirect control)

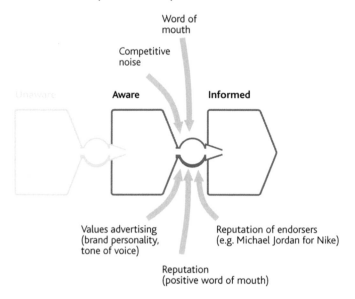

Management levers (direct control)

From informed to quality perceivers

A fraction of informed individuals will be influenced to move further along the choice chain to perceive the brand as being of high quality (Exhibit 2.6).

Quality perception has two aspects: tangible (concerned with the quality of the product) and intangible (concerned with the quality of the image). Quality is a subjective assessment; my notion of quality will differ from yours. As might be expected, quality perception is a prerequisite to choice. Our research indicates that people won't choose a service or product if they don't associate the brand proposition with a degree of quality they find satisfactory.[1] Being "OK" is not good enough.

For many brands in many industries, only half of an original sample of 1,000 people will actually make it to the stage of quality perceivers. The rest get "stuck" at earlier stages in the customer choice chain.

In much the same way, a fraction of quality perceivers will reside at this stage for some time until the dynamics of the market (or the brand owner's marketing efforts) move them along the chain to become users, or back

Exhibit 2.6
The transition from informed to quality perceivers
Examples of external factors and management levers

External factors (indirect control)

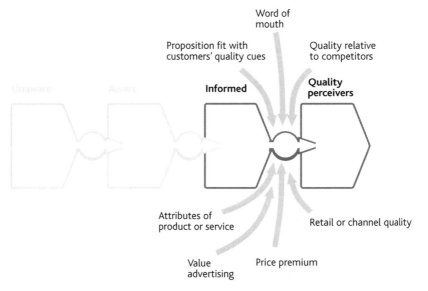

Management levers (direct control)

along the chain and out of the system. These "residing" quality perceivers in fact represent an under-utilized resource. They are valuable because they already perceive brand quality, and it is likely that the brand owner has spent money and used resources to get them to this stage, but they have failed to make the vital next step to becoming users. For those with an operational cast of mind, they are comparable to an inventory of half-finished goods.

From quality perceivers to users

Quality perceivers who also regard the brand as good value for money typically form the core of those who will move on to become users, given the right incentives (Exhibit 2.7). Companies constantly seek ways of converting quality perceivers into users. Product innovation is a common example. For instance, when Colgate launches a new toothpaste such as Fresh Confidence, part of its purpose is to entice quality perceivers to make the transition to actual usage. It hopes to achieve this aim by offering new combinations of benefits such as whiter teeth and fresher breath as well as cavity protection.

Exhibit 2.7
The transition from quality perceivers to users
Examples of external factors and management levers

External factors (indirect control)

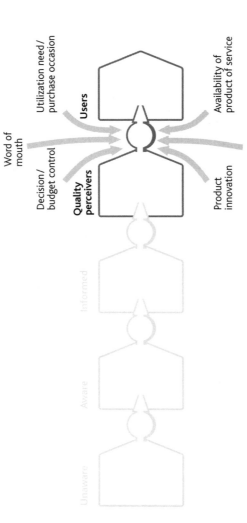

Word of mouth

Utilization need/ purchase occasion

Decision/ budget control

Users

Quality perceivers

Availability of product of service

Product innovation

Trial (samples, sales promotions, discounts)

Informed

Aware

Unaware

Management levers (direct control)

Within the user category there may be several sub-populations: for instance, exclusive (loyal) users and non-exclusive (disloyal) users (those who use other brands from the same category at the same time). A consumer might use several soft-drink brands but only one detergent brand, or *vice versa*.

Usage should not be confused with trial. Trialing, as with a promotional offer, is a management lever applied to convert non-users into users. It is not a stage in the customer choice chain. Having tried a brand, people might not be satisfied with the experience and thus not consider themselves users.

Clearly, users are essential to a company; it is they who, accumulated, are the source of the revenues generated by the brand up until today. In some industries, such as consumer goods, the bulk of revenues may come from the existing stock of users, whose repeat purchases make up a large proportion of sales. In other sectors, such as consumer durables or emerging technologies, sales may chiefly stem from an inflow of first-time buyers. Some sectors derive numerous sales from the kind of random usage that occurs when customers make impulse purchases from a retailer, or walk into a fast-food restaurant they happen to be passing.

When a company compares the value it obtains from customers with the cost of acquiring them, it will typically identify a fraction of customers that are costing it money. This often leads to a management debate about whether to keep or decline these customers' patronage. But in fact the real debate lies elsewhere.

Perhaps the company lacks the ability to justify a price premium to this segment. Perhaps it is neglecting to explore options for creating value with these customers through targeted propositions or fee-based services. Then again, it may be taking an unfocused approach to segmentation and failing to attract the right kind of customers who will generate value for the proposition. Or, as we will see later, it may simply be that it is disproportionately costly to keep these customers in the franchise.

In most industries and categories, the fact that a customer has used a product or service in the past is not a reliable indicator that they will choose it again next time. The real source of sustainable value is to be found in the next stage of the choice chain: people who not only use your brand but declare they will certainly choose it again next time they make a purchase from its category.

From users to convinced

Probably the most important parameter in branding is the measure of how many consumers are convinced they will buy the brand again. It is what we call conviction, or the certain future choice of the brand (Exhibit 2.8).

Exhibit 2.8
The transition from users to convinced
Examples of external factors and management levers

External factors (indirect control)

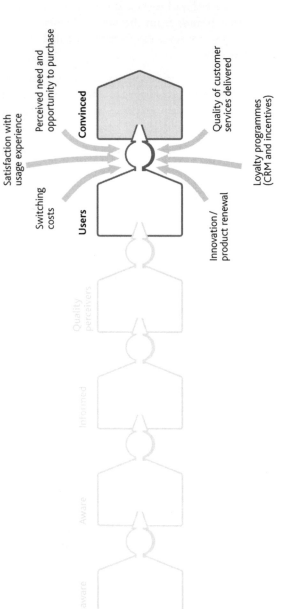

Satisfaction with
usage experience

Perceived need and
opportunity to purchase

Switching
costs

Convinced

Quality of customer
services delivered

Users

Innovation/
product renewal

Loyalty programmes
(CRM and incentives)

Quality
perceivers

Informed

Aware

Unaware

Management levers (direct control)

No one can predict with certainty that people will actually choose a given brand to the exclusion of competing brands. However, it *is* possible to determine how predisposed people are to choose a particular brand next time they make a choice within its category. In most businesses focused on end customers and consumers, these individuals will represent the main source of future cash flows.

For most brands, "convinced" consumers are people who have already used the value proposition, have been satisfied, and state that they will certainly choose it again next time. By "value proposition," we mean here the total set of real and perceived tangible and intangible benefits delivered relative to the "hurdles" in terms of the price, complexity, and time involved in obtaining that proposition.

There are several sub-categories of "convinced" customers, of which four are especially important:

Exclusively convinced, or Loyals: past users who state they will certainly choose the brand in question (and no other competing brand) next time they make a choice within its category.

Multiple convinced, or Disloyals: past users who state they will certainly choose the brand as well as other competing brands next time they make a choice within its category.

Virtual convinced, or Virtuals: people who state they will certainly choose the brand, but who have not yet used it. They are mentally predisposed in favor of the brand and want to experience it, but have yet to do so. They may have been blocked up to now by hurdles such as price or distribution, or they may simply be waiting for the right moment. Far too often this group is dismissed as irrelevant, but in some industries it can be very important. In luxury brands, for instance, virtuals make up a big slice of next-time purchasers. A young man may well become a "virtual convinced" of Porsche at 18, but wait for years before becoming an actual user.

Negatively convinced, or Refusers: people who state they will certainly not choose the brand in future. Whether they have used the brand or not, they have some reason for rejecting it. Most people can probably think of several brands they have no intention of buying. Perhaps they have bought a brand in the past and found it disappointing, or perhaps they associate it with businesses or practices they consider unethical, such as tobacco, oil, or sweatshop manufacturing methods.

Our research has revealed some hard-to-swallow facts for brand owners. First, it turns out that as many as two-thirds of all brands generate more refusers (people who are not just indifferent but ardently opposed) than convinced. Second, the ratio of refusers to convinced can be very high, ranging from 2 to 50.

Refusers can be created by a number of factors, all of which point to a company's failure to compete effectively in its chosen game. They include active dislike of what the company stands for or the nature of its products or services; the mismanagement of expectations or value delivery; poor customer understanding and segmentation; or inappropriate use of communication and marketing initiatives for different segments.

Clearly, a high ratio of refusers to convinced represents inefficiencies in generating customer choice. Worse, refusers represent a pool of people with a propensity to spread negative word of mouth (*see* text panel).

Word of mouth

Most marketers recognize word of mouth – sometimes referred to as viral marketing – as a potentially important lever. The key questions to answer are: How is it generated? Where does it have an impact? How much of an impact does it have?

As an example of positive word of mouth, consider the horror film *The Blair-Witch Project*. It tells the tale of three student filmmakers who disappear in a wood while shooting a documentary. A year later, their footage is found – but not them. This modern-day shocker was made on a tight budget, and instead of spending millions on promoting it, the makers used the web to spread the idea that it was a real-life story. So effective was the word of mouth that people flocked to see it.

The advent of the web has increased the power of negative word of mouth too. McDonald's decision to sue two environmental activists for libel in the mid 1990s resulted in one of the longest trials in English history. Although the company eventually won, the trial generated so much negative word of mouth that its image was tarnished. The McSpotlight website continues to criticize the brand.

From convinced to ambassadors

Ambassadors, as the word suggests, are positive advocates of a brand (Exhibit 2.9).

The importance of having or creating ambassadors for a brand has prompted much debate in marketing. Although creating ambassadors should always be part of any brand's strategic ambition, it is nevertheless more of an aspiration than an achievable feat. Our research shows that for most brands, ambassadors are a small group of people who are difficult to cultivate.

Exhibit 2.9
The transition from convinced to ambassadors
Examples of external factors and management levers

External factors (indirect control)

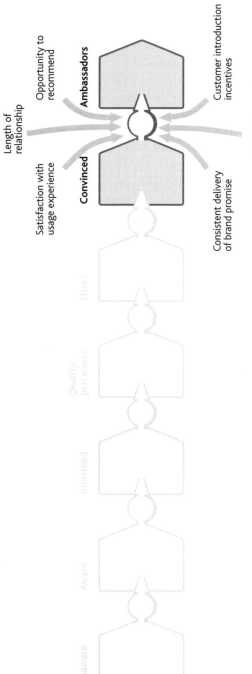

Length of
relationship

Opportunity to
recommend

Satisfaction with
usage experience

Ambassadors

Convinced

Customer introduction
incentives

Consistent delivery
of brand promise

Ability to exceed
customer expectations

Unaware

Aware

Informed

Quality
perceivers

Users

Management levers (direct control)

Exhibit 2.10
Understanding the drivers of choice

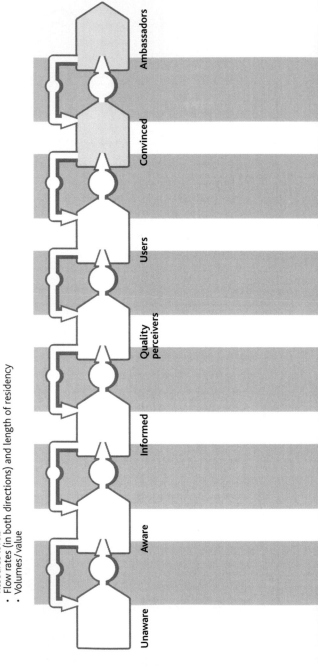

Horizontal – Strategic focus
Brand and business performance
- Resource levels
- Flow rates (in both directions) and length of residency
- Volumes / value

Unaware Aware Informed Quality perceivers Users Convinced Ambassadors

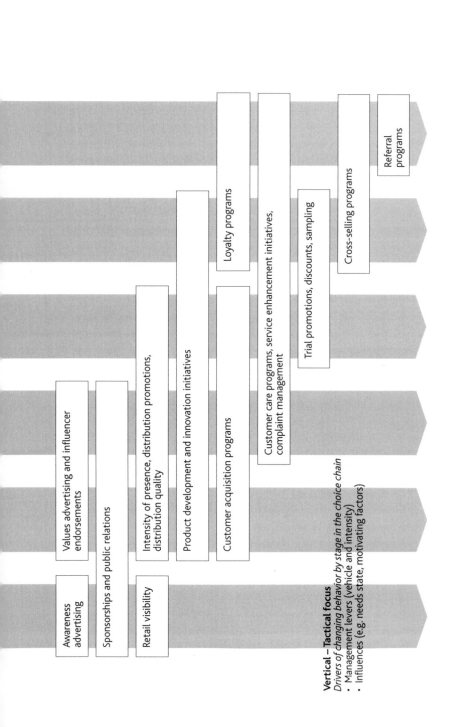

Awareness
advertising

Values advertising and influencer
endorsements

Sponsorships and public relations

Retail visibility

Intensity of presence, distribution promotions,
distribution quality

Product development and innovation initiatives

Loyalty programs

Customer acquisition programs

Customer care programs, service enhancement initiatives,
complaint management

Trial promotions, discounts, sampling

Cross-selling programs

Referral
programs

Vertical – Tactical focus
Drivers of changing behavior by stage in the choice chain
• Management levers (vehicle and intensity)
• Influences (e.g. needs state, motivating factors)

Getting a fuller picture

The customer choice chain as we have described it is necessarily a generalized one. In practice, companies need to tailor their own choice chain for their particular industry and brand, and analyze it according to the segments that are most relevant to them. However, the key pieces of information they will need for strategy development and performance measurement are common to all customer chains. These are: the number of people residing at each stage in the chain; their value or volume patterns; and the factors that drive them to progress along the chain, along with the management tools that influence these movements.

As we have seen, it is not just marketing that drives customer choice, but a combination of functions including product development, distribution, and human resources. Exhibit 2.10 gives an overview of the management levers that can be used to influence customers' behavior at different stages in the choice chain.

The issues managers and marketers face in building and sustaining their brands often revolve around a common set of themes:

Where should we focus to source growth?

• What makes customers in different markets and segments choose our brand?

• Which of our customers are defecting, and to which competing brands? Which customers can we attract from competing brands?

• How should we divide our attention between customer acquisition management and customer retention management?

• Are we sufficiently responsive to market dynamics? Do we switch priorities quickly as conditions change?

How much should we invest in brand building, and in what activities?

• Are our brand-building investments effective? What returns do they achieve?

• How much do we need to spend simply to keep our brand system in a steady state?

• What are the management levers we should invest in to achieve our performance objectives?

Do we have the appropriate systems and structures in place to manage the process?

- Do we have the facts we need to make well-informed and robust strategic and tactical decisions?

- What are the key lead indicators and brand performance measures we should be monitoring?

- Is our organization appropriately aligned – for instance, in terms of management style, skills, mindset, and staff incentives – to deliver the strategy?

If you too are struggling with questions like these, a clear view of your brand system and the drivers of choice in your customer chain will provide the basis for a sound response, as the following chapters will show.

Notes

1 See also chapter 4 on value systems and fit.

3

Balancing
stakeholder
choices

Main themes

- The brand is not a single asset. The brand and the business are two sides of the same system.

- There is a choice chain for each of a brand's stakeholders. Stakeholders are free agents acting under their own volition. Their choice of your brand doesn't materialize automatically and can't be taken for granted. Even so, stakeholders represent important resources in the business system.

- As with customer choice, a company has to compete continuously for stakeholders' choices of its brand. Just as it manages customers, so it must manage each stakeholder choice chain to earn continuing choice.

- Stakeholders contribute to a company's business in exchange for the value that it delivers to them. So when it thinks about creating value with brands, a company must in fact think about delivering value to stakeholders. For this value delivery to be feasible, the company needs to secure *symmetrical* stakeholder choice

- Competing for choice is fundamental. It is relevant for all industries, all sectors, and all markets (except monopolies). However, different industries compete for choice in different ways according to the degree of dependency between their stakeholders.

To sustain performance over time, a company must earn the symmetrical choice of all stakeholders.

Just as there is a choice chain for customers, there are similar chains for the other stakeholders of a company, including:

Skilled employees. Many companies are familiar with the "war for talent" – the need to compete for the choice of the best employees at every point in the organization, from customer service to innovation, IT to management.

Keen investors. To secure operating and growth capital, a company typically needs to earn and sustain the choice of the right investors with the right long-term outlook.

Strong partners. To establish effective manufacturing and distribution, a company needs to attract and earn the preferential choice of high-caliber strategic and operational partners.

Depending on the industry, other individuals or organizations may also be stakeholders: governments, local authorities, alumni, interest groups, and so on.

Consider how choice is exercised by employees. They are likely to be attracted to work for a company with a brand that they know is instantly recognizable, that represents values that they share, and that they trust will provide superior professional and personal benefits. A "well-branded" employer such as Harvard University or Coca-Cola or GE will find it easier to attract the choices of top talent because of the prestige attached to its brand.

Mark Wade, sustainable development manager at Shell International, explains how this works in practice:

> When you come to customers, feeling good about a company is the number one determinant of consumer choice. Of course price and other aspects of the mix have to be right but there are deeper feelings. People are increasingly making choices and buying from or doing business with companies that they feel reflect their wider expectations and values.
>
> That applies to recruitment as well – both graduates and more senior people are increasingly attracted to Shell because they see an organization in transformation and one that is serious about its commitments. And governments too – it helps if they believe you can contribute to their strategic energy needs and help grow their economies in a responsible way that takes care of the environment and helps to build social capacity.
>
> If you put all these things together, if people believe you are serious about doing things properly, it enhances your reputation – and it becomes self-reinforcing. You get the virtuous circle – so long as your performance genuinely supports the reputation."[1]

It is easy to see how these principles apply to knowledge-based industries founded on innovation and intellectual property. But they also hold good for service industries and consumer-focused companies, where the skills of service staff are crucial.

A company such as Coca-Cola would naturally like to see talented employees choose to work for it, value-seeking investors buy shares in it, strong partners work with it, and millions of consumers purchase its products. Looked at another way, a consumer will choose to drink Coca-Cola, an employee to work for Coca-Cola, a distribution partner to be associated with Coca-Cola, and an investor to put money into Coca-Cola. The brand is the focal point for each stakeholder and each choice (Exhibit 3.1).

Exhibit 3.1
Stakeholder choice chains

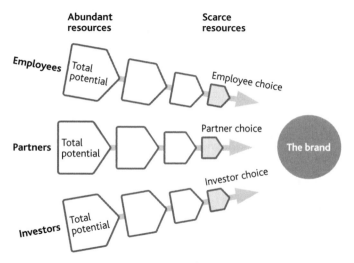

Needless to say, stakeholders vary from one industry to another. However, the stakeholder choice chain is relevant to any organization. Universities have their alumni, professors, government, sponsors, and so on; charities have their donors; and political parties have their members, supporters, and electorate.

Like customer choice chains, stakeholder choice chains are also *scarcity* chains: though the overall number of *potential* employees, investors, and partners may be considerable, the number who actually *choose* a particular company or brand is limited. It follows that segmenting stakeholders and applying the right management levers is just as important as it is for customers. While some companies regard, say, employees as a limitless pool of individuals, other more sophisticated organizations take steps to segment potential employees. They may, for instance, select their trainees from a handful of the most prestigious universities, so creating a hurdle that narrows down the segment from which they seek to earn choice, just as companies with premium brands use price to help define their target customer segments.

The symmetry of stakeholder choice

Any stakeholder choice chain represents a number of people who act from different motives, with different means, and according to different time horizons. In addition, the various stakeholders influence each other across the choice chains. So it's vital to understand not only each individual stakeholder's perspective but also the dynamics within and between each choice chain.

All investments in management initiatives – marketing, new product development, packaging, plant development, distribution systems, professional development – contribute to getting a given brand chosen by its stakeholders. What's crucial is that all these stakeholder choices are in balance. We call this the symmetry of stakeholder choice (Exhibit 3.2).

Exhibit 3.2
The symmetry of stakeholder choice

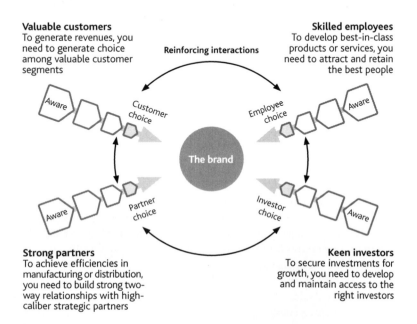

Valuable customers
To generate revenues, you need to generate choice among valuable customer segments

Skilled employees
To develop best-in-class products or services, you need to attract and retain the best people

Reinforcing interactions

Aware · Customer choice · Employee choice · Aware

The brand

Aware · Partner choice · Investor choice · Aware

Strong partners
To achieve efficiencies in manufacturing or distribution, you need to build strong two-way relationships with high-caliber strategic partners

Keen investors
To secure investments for growth, you need to develop and maintain access to the right investors

Consider what happens if the stakeholders are *not* in balance. If a company has talented employees to help it innovate, but fails to win customers with a relevant proposition, it will have little chance of sustaining a successful business. The same will be true if, conversely, it has eager customers but lacks skilled employees to produce innovative new products or provide the right level of service. Admittedly, companies do extricate themselves from predicaments like these, but seldom without suffering a period of poor performance. Indeed, in cases where they aren't able to compete for investors' choices, they can even be driven out of business.

Central to the idea of symmetrical stakeholder choice is the recognition that the brand is the interface between the company and its stakeholders – the focal point for competing for the choice of each stakeholder.

To illustrate this, let's look at how stakeholder choice chains combine with various other resources to make up a company's business system. Revenues are driven by the number of customers who actually choose the brand multiplied by the frequency with which they choose it multiplied by the

Exhibit 3.3
Stakeholder choice chains and the P&L

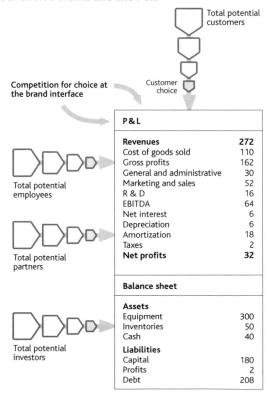

P&L	
Revenues	272
Cost of goods sold	110
Gross profits	162
General and administrative	30
Marketing and sales	52
R & D	16
EBITDA	64
Net interest	6
Depreciation	6
Amortization	18
Taxes	2
Net profits	**32**

Balance sheet	
Assets	
Equipment	300
Inventories	50
Cash	40
Liabilities	
Capital	180
Profits	2
Debt	208

Total potential customers

Competition for choice at the brand interface

Customer choice

Total potential employees

Total potential partners

Total potential investors

price that they are prepared to pay. So the customer choice chain is in fact the revenue-generating choice chain on the company's P&L.

Exhibit 3.3 shows in schematic form how stakeholder choice chains relate to the P&L as typically represented. At the top, the customer choice chain drives revenues. On the left, the employee choice chain provides human resources and skills such as marketing capabilities, while the partner choice chain contributes facilities such as retail distribution. Both of these influence the cost side of the P&L. The investor choice chain influences the balance sheet through capital provision.

Common to each of these stakeholder choice chains is the brand interface. The stakeholders are free agents who can move along the choice chain of their own free will, selecting the company's brand or someone else's. The challenge for the company is therefore to sustain performance by earning scarce stakeholder choices on a continual basis.

Note that the boundary of the company doesn't end at the resources itemized in the balance sheet. Loyal customers, employees, and so on are

Exhibit 3.4
The brand and the business: Two sides of the same system

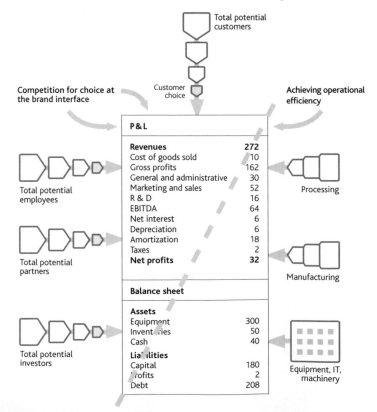

key elements in the resource system even though they aren't "owned" by the company or captured in classic managerial accounting measurements.

Other physical and operational resources influence the cost side of the P&L. A paper pulp company, for example, will have a chain that starts with planting trees, progresses to mature trees, and then goes on to logs ready for processing. For a manufacturing company, the chain will typically move from components to end products. Pharmaceutical companies have an R&D pipeline with stages of clinical trial before launch. The scarcity in these instances tends to arise through wastage or inefficiencies during processing. A series of other static resources – plant, manufacturing equipment, and so on – also influences the balance sheet.

Exhibit 3.4 shows how these resources link in to the P&L and balance sheet. Stakeholder chains are on one side, operational resources on the other. The management focus for the first lies in competing for choice; for the second, in achieving operational efficiency. When we look at the system in this way, it becomes clear that the brand and the business are indeed two interdependent parts of a single system (*see* text panel, "What are systems?")

What are systems?

The *New Oxford Dictionary of English* defines a system as "a set of things working together as parts of a mechanism or an interconnecting network."

Whether something is defined as a system or a resource depends on one's perspective. Machinery is a resource from a management standpoint, for instance, but it probably looks like a system to the engineer who has to maintain it.

A simple way to classify a system is by its degree of complexity (how many components does it have? How much does a change in one component affect other parts of the system?) and by the extent to which its parts interact with those of other systems (is it "open" or "closed"?).

Take the human body. It is a system with a relatively high degree of complexity: a malfunction in one part of the body is likely to have repercussions in others. It is also a fairly closed system (but not entirely closed, as it interacts with the outside environment in a number of ways).

In a company, the brand and the business are two sides of one interdependent system. The company cannot function without the interaction of such resources as value proposition, customers, staff, cash, and reputation. To view a brand as a single asset is not just misguided, but positively dangerous for strategy development.

Value delivery

To earn the choice of stakeholders, a brand must deliver value to them in return. What represents value to an individual in any of the choice chains is a subjective combination of real and perceived tangible and intangible benefits.

For a customer buying a product, for example, value delivery will typically include a combination of tangible attributes (such as quality and functionality) and intangible attributes (such as image, trust, liking, and feeling), as well as auxiliary components (such as current users). All these elements are bundled in the branded value proposition. Consumers then evaluate these benefits in relation to the *hurdles* of obtaining the value proposition (including price, time to acquire or experience, and complexity in taking delivery) before choosing (or refusing) the value delivery.

Depending on whether value delivery met expectations and was distinctive relative to competing propositions, customers may be willing to choose the brand again next time they experience a need for a product within that category. Meanwhile, management will seek to apply levers such as communications or product development to improve the perceived value as against the hurdles, and thus increase the probability of choice.

All stakeholders will evaluate the value provision or delivery in relation to competing provisions. Value delivery to employees is likely to be a combination of factors including salary, professional development, interesting assignments, community, security, and pride. To partners, it is pay, market and consumer intelligence, IP (intellectual property), and reputation. To investors, it includes consistent financial performance in terms of share price and dividends as well as corporate ethics and trust. Exhibit 3.5 shows how a company delivers value to stakeholders to earn their choices.

As we have seen, a company must compete effectively for scarce choices *and* achieve operational effectiveness in developing or acquiring relatively abundant inanimate resources. When accomplished in appropriate sequence and measure, the two aspects combine to create a self-reinforcing virtuous cycle that enables the company to provide value to *all* its stakeholders.

Underpinning this view is the recognition that it is fundamentally flawed to treat a brand as an isolated asset. The brand and the business are in reality two parts of a single integrated resource system.

It is easy to see how this works if we imagine a company wanting to sell a well-known consumer goods brand. In the unlikely event that, say,

Exhibit 3.5
Delivering value to stakeholders

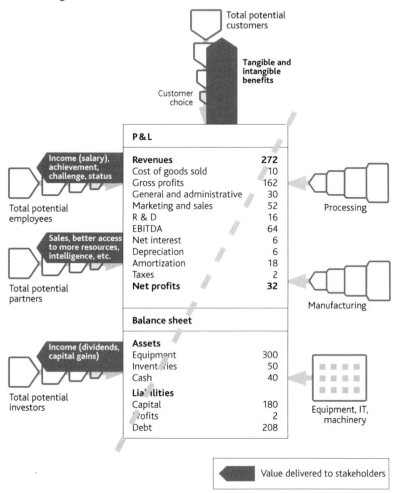

Kellogg's should decide to sell its brand, it would be selling not just the Kellogg's trademark but also a whole series of resources including the millions of loyal customers who choose to eat Kellogg's for breakfast every morning, and perhaps even the staff, the distributors, and so on (Exhibit 3.6).

Many people mistake the trademark for the brand. A trademark is in fact an asset, just like plant and equipment; what it is *not* is another name for a brand.

Just as a business isn't a single asset, neither is a brand. While business and brand aren't one and the same thing, they are nevertheless inextricably intertwined: in a competitive market, neither can exist without the other.

Exhibit 3.6
The brand as a resource system
Hypothetical example: Kellogg's

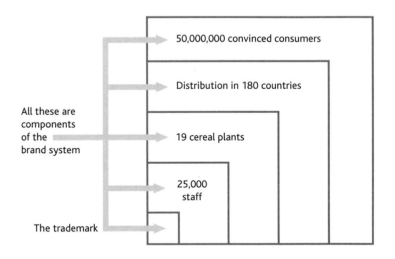

All these are
components
of the
brand system

50,000,000 convinced consumers

Distribution in 180 countries

19 cereal plants

25,000
staff

The trademark

For anyone who develops business or brand strategy, or manages a business or a brand, it is critical to recognize, understand, and quantify the full set of resources that make up the brand system.

Choice dependency

Competing effectively for choice is critical for any organization, regardless of industry or sector.[2] Exhibit 3.7 depicts four different types of environment within which companies compete for customer choice. Each is characterized by the degree of dependency that exists between stakeholders in order that a brand can earn customer choice and thus generate revenue.

Branded retailers such as Gap, Benetton, and Zara have direct **independent** access to the end customer through their own outlets. On the plus side, this gives them more control over the content, style, and speed of brand delivery; on the minus side, it may be expensive to operate. By contrast, most consumer goods manufacturers deliver their products through retail intermediaries. This means that the brand operates through two **interdependent** choice chains because the customer must first choose a retailer in order then to choose the brand.

Exhibit 3.7
The choice dependency matrix

Dependency on stakeholder choices for realization of brand choice in different industries (simplified)

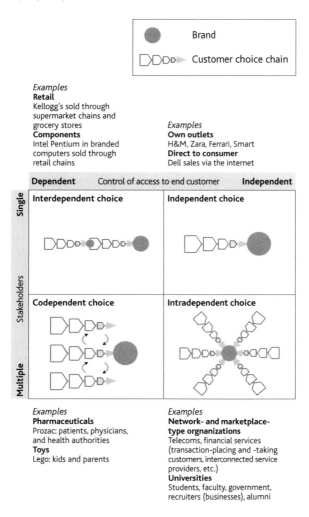

Some companies use both of these methods. Nike has its own Nike Town stores to give it direct independent access to customer choice, but it also distributes its products through branded retailers.

In some industries, stakeholder choice is **codependent**: the combined choice of each stakeholder is required before the choice can materialize. In pharmaceuticals, prescription drugs such as Zoton, Prozac, and Viagra must be jointly chosen by health authorities, doctors, and patients before usage and repeat choices become possible. The same principle applies to toys such as Lego and Nintendo: in many cases, both parents and children have to agree on a choice prior to purchase.

Finally, network- and marketplace-type companies compete in an environment of **intradependent** choice, where each individual or organization that makes a choice becomes an important component of the overall value proposition. Examples include online auctioneers, financial service firms, and telecoms companies with transaction-placing and transaction-taking customers.

A company's field of choice dependency may not be static. Some businesses take deliberate steps to move to different positions within the matrix as they explore new business models to create new operating environments and opportunities. However, each type of choice environment is characterized by different skill sets, scale economies, and operating models.

Early in 2000, consumer goods company Unilever attempted to move into the direct independent choice model with a new proposition targeted directly at consumers. Called myHome and piloted in South London, it consisted of a laundrette and home cleaning service intended to build on the strength of the Persil and Jif (now Cif) brands. However, Unilever subsequently decided that it would take too long to make the new business scalable, and put it up for sale in autumn 2001.

Having a strong brand and a distinctive value proposition is not enough. A successful business must also be clear about its system of stakeholders, whether and how they depend on one another, and the drivers of choice for each stakeholder at each stage in the choice chain.

However, choice doesn't materialize automatically out of these structures. There are certain prerequisites for successful branding that must be in place before management can focus on the finer points of achieving choice effectively.

If a company is to decode and optimize the interdependencies within the system that determine its performance, it will need a management approach with skills and structures that can accommodate these dynamics, as we shall see in the next chapter.

Notes

1 Roger Cowe, "Fuelling opinion," Identity Matters, 18, Spring 2002, pp. 10–11.

2 This is also the case for non-profit organizations, with the difference that they don't usually have investors; if they do, these investors are seeking value in forms other than financial gain.

4

Managing the
dynamics of brand
architecture

Main themes

- Most of the metrics managers currently employ to track and manage brand performance are inadequate.

- The brand and business system is dynamic, with leverage for each choice segment constantly shifting. Moreover, there is a natural tendency for resources in the system to decay. As a result, investments must be made merely to sustain the status quo; you have to run just to stand still.

- To leverage under-utilized resources and allocate brand-building investments effectively, managers must apply accurate and detailed performance intelligence. This will allow them to make informed decisions and target initiatives at key leverage points in the system.

- Understanding the performance of a business is not just about grasping the factual metrics of the brand architecture, but also about establishing the prerequisites for successful branding and responding to consumer values as they evolve over time

- The brand management debate must be refocused. Classic marketing discussions based on past brand performance and consumer awareness levels get companies nowhere. Instead, they need to adopt a holistic view of the integrated brand and business system. This should allow them to answer a number of tough management questions. It will also reveal that there are far more opportunities for management to take initiatives to optimize performance than most businesses recognize.

Applying a holistic and systemic approach to brand management will help managers develop more robust strategy, make investments in the right initiatives, and align the organization to compete more effectively for stakeholder choices.

Since the value of a business lies in the whole system, companies need to be effective at building and leveraging *all* the resources in the system to optimize value creation. For too long, managers have focused primarily on tangible resources simply because they are easily quantifiable and often appear in management reporting. In the process, they have largely neglected other resources such as the number of convinced consumers, the state of staff morale, and other "soft" or knowledge-based assets such as patents and skills. Starved of management attention, such resources are under-utilized in many companies.

To establish a solid foundation for brand growth, managers need to start by understanding what the brand is about, where it can be taken, and what market and consumer opportunities exist (*see* text panel, "What are brands?").

What are brands?

Attempts to pin down exactly what a brand is have been many and various. Consider the following:

"A brand is a name, term, sign, symbol, or design, or a combination of them, intended to identify the goods or services of one seller or group of sellers and to differentiate them from those of competition."

American Marketing Association[1]

"A brand is a complex symbol. It is the intangible sum of a product's attributes, its name, packaging, and price, its history, reputation, and the way it is advertised. A brand is also defined by consumers' impressions of the people who use it, as well as their own experience."

Advertising guru David Ogilvy, 1955

"It is people who call brands into existence – who form attachments, detest homogeneity, value consistency and delight in conferring personality characteristics on animals, entities and inanimate objects. People have been confidently differentiating between objects since they were first invited to make a choice between two identical arrowheads."

Niall FitzGerald, CEO, Unilever[2]

This chapter focuses on three areas central to brand and business performance comprehension and management:

- The prerequisites for successful branding: articulating the key strategic choices to be made to earn stakeholder choice. The perspective on growth must be market-driven and "outside in" (where and how can we source what growth?) rather than "inside out" (setting year-on-year growth targets irrespective of brand resources).

- The brand architecture: mapping, quantifying, and understanding both the system and the leverage opportunities within it. Intangible resources are integral to this process; they can make all the difference to competitive performance.

- Values systems: aligning brand and stakeholder values to ensure value creation.

The CEO must understand and integrate all three in order to develop and implement a robust brand growth strategy.

We believe none of these definitions fully captures the essence of a brand; rather, the attributes they describe belong to specific resources within the wider brand system. To obtain an accurate picture of what a brand is, most people will need to stop seeing the brand as a single asset and start seeing it as a resource system. This calls for a complete change in mindset.

The key characteristics of a brand can be summarized as follows:

- It is a resource system: the totality of tangible and intangible components that are both internal and external to the company.

- It is a focal point for all stakeholders: the embodiment of the company, its image, and its values, or the "face" it presents to the world.

- It is the basis for competing for the choice of current and potential stakeholders: the manifest representation of the business and its total value proposition.

- It is a promise to these stakeholders and also a responsibility to keep that promise, making the brand owner an accountable entity in the wider society.

The prerequisites for successful branding

A company cannot set out to brand simply because it wants to. Stakeholders' choice of a brand has to be earned, just as politicians have to win elections before they can hold office. But elections happen only every few years, whereas a company must earn its customers' choices day in, day out.

There are four interdependent prerequisites for successful branding, each of which implies a series of strategic choices for management:

- **Establish a clear strategic principle.** Management must clearly articulate the mission, vision, and values of the company and brand, and embed them in the organization so as to align and focus every person within it on competing for choice. It must clarify why it wants to brand and define its target markets and segments in the light of the changing environment.

- **Provide a distinctive value proposition.** The company must develop and consistently deliver a value proposition that is distinctive, attractive, and relevant to the intended segment so as to earn customers' choices, secure repeat purchases, and justify the price premium.

- **Control core resources in the value chain.** The company must develop and leverage the resources (ideally proprietary ones) that it needs to deliver the value proposition. These resources often include aspects of systems, skills, structures, and intellectual property that are applied to build and leverage unique competitive advantage and to prevent or inhibit the copying of products or practices by rival players.

- **Proactively manage stakeholder relationships.** The company must engage in real two-way relationships that enable it to communicate effectively and to capture learning in order to enhance its value proposition.

Exhibit 4.1 shows how these four elements interrelate to inform and develop one another so that a company can earn choice on a continuous basis. This dynamic process fosters innovation and drives business renewal.

The benefits provided by a proposition often have to do with resolving a real or perceived customer problem or need on the one hand, or providing or inducing an experience that is perceived as positive by the customer on the other. The extent to which these benefits are delivered is important to future repurchases and positive word of mouth, but there is a delicate balance to be struck. Over-delivering may generate repurchases, but it can equally undermine margins. The secret is to satisfy the specific

Exhibit 4.1
The dynamics of earning choice

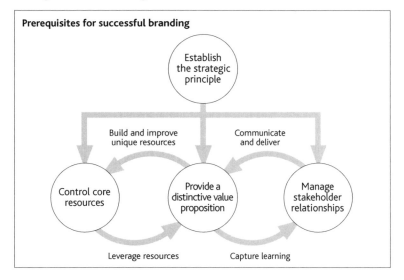

Prerequisites for successful branding

Establish the strategic principle

Build and improve unique resources

Communicate and deliver

Control core resources

Provide a distinctive value proposition

Manage stakeholder relationships

Leverage resources

Capture learning

expectations of relevant customer segments – in other words, to make the right fact-based strategic choices.

Progressive Corporation, a us vehicle insurance specialist, has a well-defined and distinctive value proposition offering a range of non-standard policies for high-risk applicants. It focuses on providing insurance to people who own motorcycles or have been charged for drunken driving, and who cannot usually obtain cover from other insurers at any price.

Whereas its competitors group all potential applicants with similar profiles into the same risk pool, Progressive conducted careful analysis of applicants' behavior, drew on its 30-year database of high-risk drivers, and identified behavior patterns that distinguish *genuinely* high-risk applicants from relatively low-risk ones. By concentrating on these relatively low-risk drivers, who would still have been classed as high-risk and refused insurance by other insurers, Progressive was able to target a niche market of its own and develop a successful high-margin business. The company uses a complex rating system to provide insurance policies that better match applicants' profiles and is able to command a price premium of up to 300 percent over the standard rate.

Since no business can be all things to all people, management must make strategic and tactical choices about how and where it wants to compete for which stakeholder choices. Exhibit 4.2 shows how the imperatives for successful branding translate into a series of detailed management choices.

Exhibit 4.2
Making strategic choices

Prerequisites for successful branding

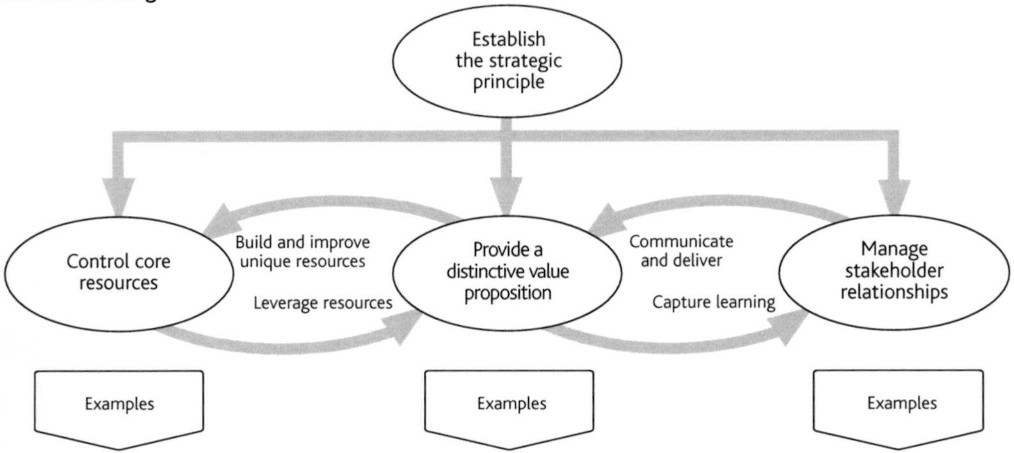

Making management choices

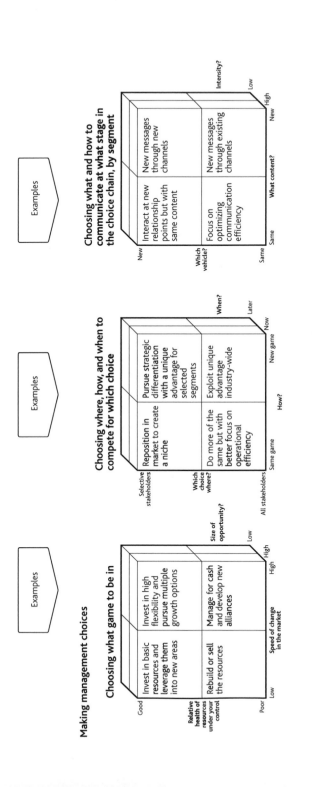

Choosing what game to be in

Relative health of resources under your control		
Good	Invest in basic resources and leverage them into new areas	Invest in high flexibility and pursue multiple growth options
Poor	Rebuild or sell the resources	Manage for cash and develop new alliances
	Low — Speed of change in the market — High	

Size of opportunity? Low / High

Examples

Choosing where, how, and when to compete for which choice

Which choice where?		
Selective stakeholders	Reposition in market to create a niche	Pursue strategic differentiation with a unique advantage for selected segments
All stakeholders	Do more of the same but with better focus on operational efficiency	Exploit unique advantage industry-wide
	Same game — How? — New game	

When? Now / Later

Examples

Choosing what and how to communicate at what stage in the choice chain, by segment

Which vehicle?		
New	Interact at new relationship points but with same content	New messages through new channels
Same	Focus on optimizing communication efficiency	New messages through existing channels
	Same — What content? — New	

Intensity? High / Low

Examples

The brand architecture

Just as builders work from architects' drawings, managers, as brand builders, should work from a brand architecture that shows how the basic building blocks – resources – fit together. Armed with a clear brand blueprint, managers will share a better understanding of their business, make better decisions about the allocation of resources, find it easier to reach consensus, and achieve better results. The blueprint will allow them to quantify the implications of the choices they make and identify the specific levers that will help them accomplish their objectives.

Exhibit 4.3 illustrates a simplified blueprint for a retail brand, showing how tangible, intangible, internal, and external resources interact within the overall system. The curved arrows show that resources (such as sales people) or management levers (such as retail promotions) can influence the flow rate of other resources (such as retail distribution).

Arguably, managing stakeholders – free agents who make up their own minds – is more complex than managing inanimate resources such as equipment or capital. Though competing for stakeholder choice may make good sense to them intuitively, most managers shy away from it, losing heart when asked to manage something that's complex, incorporates many intangible components, and can't be kicked.

What does the absence of a clear brand architecture mean for a business? When structures, facts, and a holistic perspective on stakeholder choice are lacking, managerial activity inevitably evolves in a fragmented manner around sub-components or functional areas. The typical result is a series of isolated and disconnected initiatives such as customer relationship management, loyalty-based management, process re-engineering, or knowledge management – each worthy enough in the right context, but capable of generating more work and confusion than benefit if used without regard for the system as a whole.

Whether any particular initiative can be applied successfully will depend on the status of the resource system: for example, how mature a brand is in a given market, which reflects the number of people residing at the later stages in the choice chain. Once managers have developed a clear brand architecture and quantified its hard and soft resources, they can understand how a given initiative is likely to influence performance, and to what extent, and so make informed choices about how best to allocate their investments.

Exhibit 4.4 illustrates this idea in a simplified form by contrasting two customer choice chains. The chain for a new brand shows that

Exhibit 4.3
Interactions in the brand system

Simplified retail example

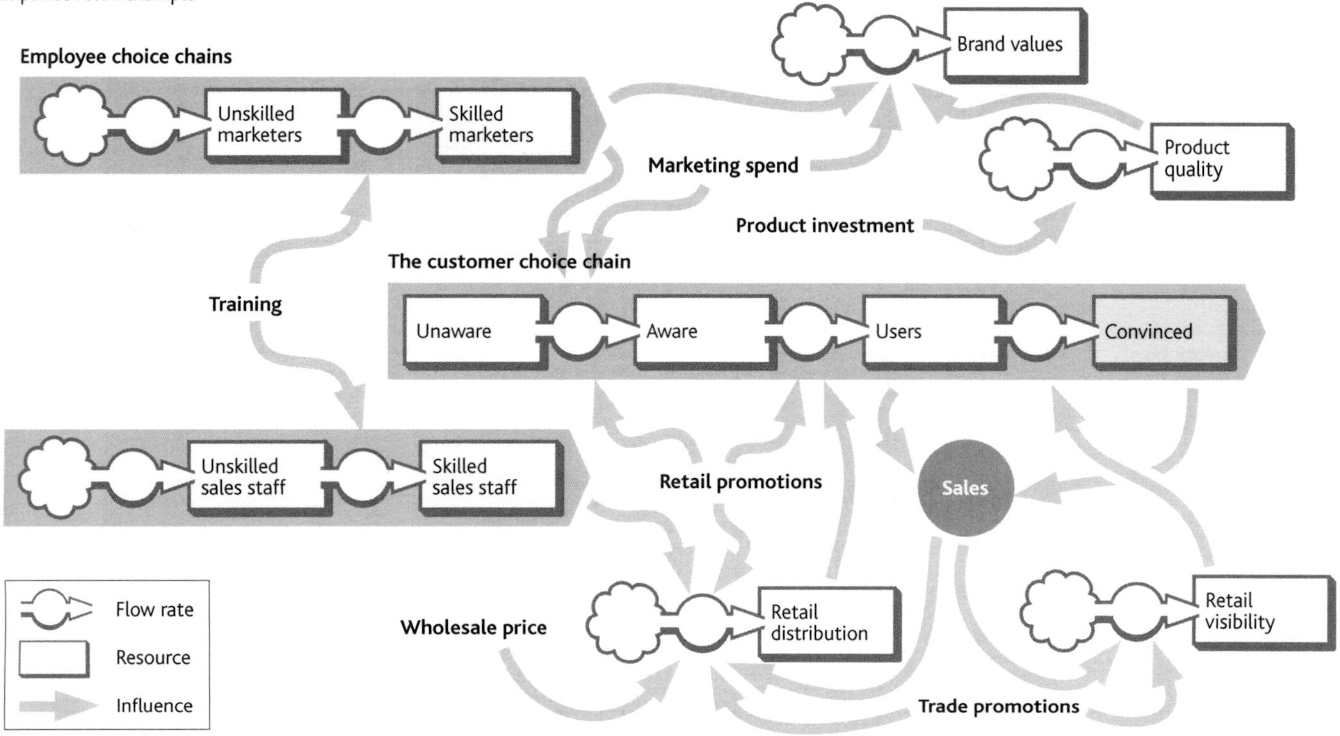

Employee choice chains

Unskilled marketers → Skilled marketers

Unskilled sales staff → Skilled sales staff

Training

The customer choice chain

Unaware → Aware → Users → Convinced

Marketing spend

Product investment

Brand values

Product quality

Retail promotions

Sales

Retail distribution

Retail visibility

Trade promotions

Wholesale price

Flow rate

Resource

Influence

Exhibit 4.4
Identifying where to focus

Scaled to 1,000

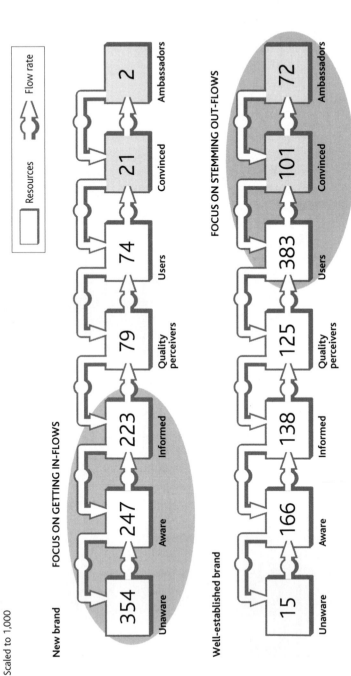

New brand   FOCUS ON GETTING IN-FLOWS

| Resources | | Flow rate |

354 Unaware — 247 Aware — 223 Informed — 79 Quality perceivers — 74 Users — 21 Convinced — 2 Ambassadors

Well-established brand

FOCUS ON STEMMING OUT-FLOWS

15 Unaware — 166 Aware — 138 Informed — 125 Quality perceivers — 383 Users — 101 Convinced — 72 Ambassadors

management needs to focus on generating in-flows in the early stages of the chain. With a well-established brand, by contrast, the focus should be on stemming out-flows in the later stages.

Experience tells us that a clear understanding of stakeholder choice chains provides the only robust platform for developing and executing strategy. Once managers are equipped with a visual plan of how the brand system works, they can have informed debates about the initiatives they might pursue and the results they can expect. The brand architecture acts as a shared language for managers from different divisions and countries, and as a basis for evaluating brand performance.

There are two caveats to bear in mind, however. First, each brand's architecture is unique. It follows that management initiatives that have worked for one brand are unlikely to work in the same way when applied to another. Copying best practice just doesn't work. The only valid basis for evaluating initiatives and making decisions is to be found within an individual brand's resource system. Any action that a company takes has to be judged in terms of the impact it will have on that system.

Second, the brand architecture is only a snapshot of the state of resources at a given moment in time. In reality, the resource system is in a constant state of flux, with constant in-flows and out-flows along the choice chains. People move along the chain as they become "convinced" – especially if management applies the right levers – but there is also a natural tendency for consumers to flow back along the chain: for instance, from "convinced" to "users." To counteract this tendency, even the best-known consumer brands have to keep up their marketing and promotional activities. If Coca-Cola stopped advertising (unthinkable though that might seem), its huge reservoirs of "convinced" consumers would gradually deplete.

Three essential components go to make up the brand architecture:

- The brand resources: tangible, intangible, animate, and inanimate.

- The interdependencies between resources: the in-flows and out-flows that influence the state or level of the resources.

- The flow drivers: the factors that influence the flow rates. These are of two types: the levers controlled by management and the external factors over which it has little or no influence.

Brand resources

Just as an architectural drawing needs a scale, a brand architecture needs to be populated with data. Most companies have abundant intelligence about their markets and customers. The trouble is, it frequently doesn't match up with the brand architecture. It isn't resource based, and it may lack crucial data such as the number of customers residing at a particular stage in the choice chain or the flow rates between different stages.

Managers need to measure resource flows before they can assess the scope of problems and opportunities for their brand. Imagine that my rate of new customers won is declining relative to my rate of customers lost. When will I see a net reduction in the customer base? I can't answer the question without knowing both flow rates.

It's not just the levels and flows of existing customers that need monitoring; tomorrow's customers are important too. For luxury brands, for example, the level of "virtual convinced" consumers and the rates of in- and out-flows of this resource are as critical as the movements of current purchasers.

Exhibit 4.5
Monitoring brand health

Flow rates are per quarter

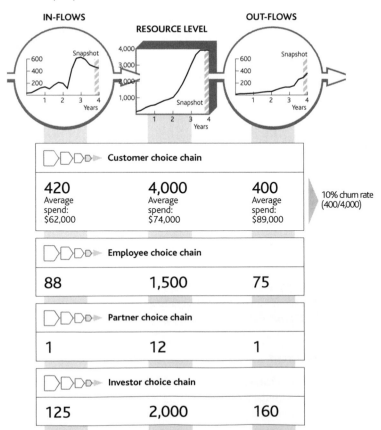

Putting numbers and values against resources, especially potential and convinced customers and their associated flows, is the only way to establish appropriate performance metrics and get an accurate picture of your brand's health. In the example illustrated in Exhibit 4.5, customer in-flows are declining while customer out-flows are rising. At the time of the "snapshot," customer in-flows are still higher than out-flows (420 new customers versus 400 lost customers this month), but the total number of customers is starting to level off as the two flows get closer to cancelling each other out.

The impact of these flows can be seen in the investor choice chain. Although 125 new investors joined this month, 160 left. Investors are losing confidence in the brand as its performance deteriorates and customers defect.

This example demonstrates the importance of measuring both levels and flows by stakeholder and segment. Indeed, this should be standard practice in any management reporting since the flow rates are lead indicators for the resource levels.

Exhibit 4.6
The impact of reducing churn
Example: US personal care brand

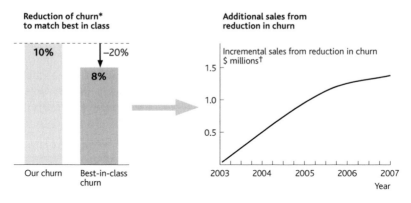

Reduction of churn*
to match best in class

10%   –20%

8%

Our churn   Best-in-class
churn

Additional sales from
reduction in churn

Incremental sales from reduction in churn
$ millions†

1.5

1.0

0.5

2003   2004   2005   2006   2007
Year

* Switches in the brand consumers use most often among
9 competing brands, taking into account average number
of switches and average time between switches

† Based on forecast sales at reduced churn

In the case of a US personal care brand, monitoring consumer flow rates allowed the brand owner to evaluate opportunities for value creation (Exhibit 4.6). Analysis of the data revealed that the brand had a churn rate (customers switching to a competing brand) of 10 percent of the customer base per year. The company carried out a benchmarking exercise with competing brands in the same price range and discovered that the best-in-class churn rate was 8 percent. It worked out how much additional value it could create by reducing churn to the best-in-class level. Finally, it weighed up the incremental sales over a given period against the costs of implementing targeted measures to reduce churn, and used the results to reach a sound fact-based decision on the right corrective actions to take.

Though this example is simplified – in reality the company would need to take into account the effects of churn-reduction measures on the rest of the brand system – it serves to illustrate how an analysis of brand resource flows can be used to support and inform management decision making.

Interdependencies between resources

Stakeholder resources are not stable; there is a continuous loss rate over time. Just as houses fall apart without maintenance, choice chains are subject to gradual decay. As a result, brands have to invest in keeping their in-flows going simply in order to maintain the status quo; they have to run just to stand still.

If a company wants to grow its customer base, it must do one of two things: *boost in-flows* so that it wins new customers at a faster rate than it loses old ones, or *reduce out-flows* so that it loses customers at a slower rate than it acquires new ones. Either way, customers accumulate and the customer base increases.

But things aren't quite as simple as this may suggest. Management must weigh up a series of issues. At what point do we step in to try and improve the flow rate to grow (customer acquisition initiatives) or to stem the decline (customer retention initiatives)? How do we determine which initiatives will influence which flow rates, and by how much? What is the right level of investment in each of these initiatives?

Breaking down the decisions in this way can yield new insights into questions that many companies grapple with: How much should we spend on marketing? Are we achieving the best possible return on our investments? However, it is important to recognize that marketing is just one of the levers that can be used to grow or retain customers' choice. Through diligent analysis, managers can ascertain what contribution marketing – as opposed to new product development, service levels, distribution, and so on – makes to the various flow rates in the customer choice chain, and thus determine how much investment is required to maintain the system in a steady state, all things being equal.

Within a resource system, as we have seen, there are in-flows (which lead to growth) and out-flows (which lead to entropy). There is also a third type of flow: migration (Exhibit 4.7). Migration takes place when a resource moves from one choice chain to another.

Exhibit 4.7
Growth, entropy, and migration

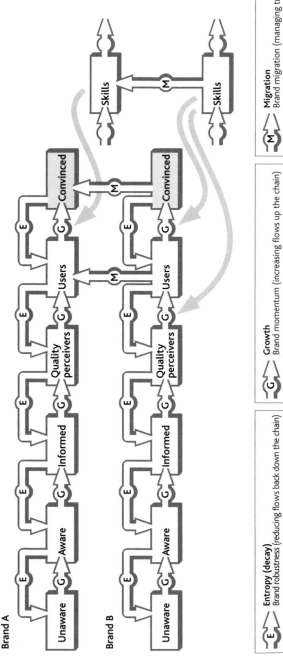

Brand A

Brand B

Unaware → Aware → Informed → Quality perceivers → Users → Convinced → Skills

E (Entropy) / G (Growth) / M (Migration)

E Entropy (decay)
Brand robustness (reducing flows back down the chain)

• What level of investment is required, and what levers will maintain or reduce it?
• How quickly will it change, and to what degree?

G Growth
Brand momentum (increasing flows up the chain)

• What level of investment is required, and what levers will maintain or reduce it?
• How quickly will it change, and to what degree?

M Migration
Brand migration (managing transitions)

• Can we migrate?
• What level of investment is required?
• How far can it be done without undermining the existing system?

Migrations typically take place in one of two settings:

When a company seeks growth in new markets or sectors. If a company wants to establish a presence in a new market where it currently has neither structures nor recognition, it will often move skilled and experienced people from an existing resource system into a new one.

When a company is trying to consolidate its business and move its customers from one brand to another. Such brand consolidation often happens in cases where two companies merge and decide to streamline their brand portfolio. Rather than abruptly discontinuing a brand, the merged entity will probably want to migrate its users across to a comparable brand that it will continue to support.

Making such transitions without diluting the existing resource base or jeopardizing the effective working of the current brand system can often be tricky.

Most brand owners and investors are quite rightly preoccupied with managing and mitigating the risks associated with the brand. As ever, understanding resource flows is the best place to start if you are assessing the robustness of your brand architecture and the performance of the system as a whole. Since revenues derive from the number of customers paying a particular price for a brand, it is the volatility of these resources that determines the risk associated with future cash flow. So it is important to gauge, for instance, how quickly "convinced" customers might defect following an unexpected mishap or market discontinuity.

Exhibit 4.8
Assessing brand risk

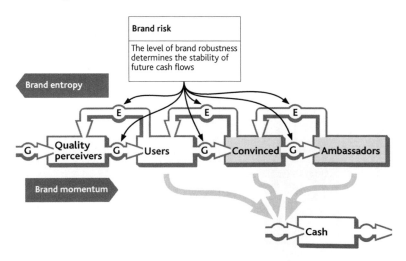

In theory, if there were no flows in or out of the customer resource nor other changes in behavior, there would be no risk associated with the brand. In practice, brand risk is a function of the stability of the resources in the customer choice chain (Exhibit 4.8). It follows that the application of management levers influences not only brand earnings but also brand risk.

Brand earnings (cash in-flow) are a function of the number of customers and the amount they spend on a brand. Brand risk reflects the volatility of this cash flow, which is determined by the out-flow of customers. A high customer out-flow would indicate a high level of uncertainty regarding future cash flows and hence high brand risk. Conversely, a company with a large number of loyal customers and low customer out-flow would enjoy high earnings, a stable cash flow, and low risk.

In 1999, people in Belgium and France complained they felt ill after consuming soft drinks manufactured by Coca-Cola. Although the company took a while to get to grips with the problem, most consumers, rather than becoming "refusers," quickly resumed consumption once it was fixed – a clear sign of the brand's robustness. Other stakeholder chains operate in much the same way. For instance, investors are more likely to stay with a company for the long haul if it enjoys the confidence of other stakeholders, as Warren Buffet attests.

Management levers

Actions taken to influence a brand system will produce a reaction at some point within it. Even if *no* actions are taken, initiatives pursued by competitors or changes elsewhere in the environment will cause reactions in the system and thus affect performance.

In short, the brand system is dynamic, and understanding its dynamics is essential to managing performance over time. Several consequences follow from this:

- Actions taken today may have immediate and/or long-term impact.

- Actions taken today will produce a different outcome from the same actions taken in the past or the future.

- The same actions taken in different markets will produce different outcomes.

- The same actions taken at the same time for different brands will produce different outcomes even within the same product category.

- Doing nothing will influence performance too.

The case of us telecom hosting company Exodus Communications demonstrates the importance of staying alert to the dynamics of the

Exhibit 4.9
Management levers and influencing factors

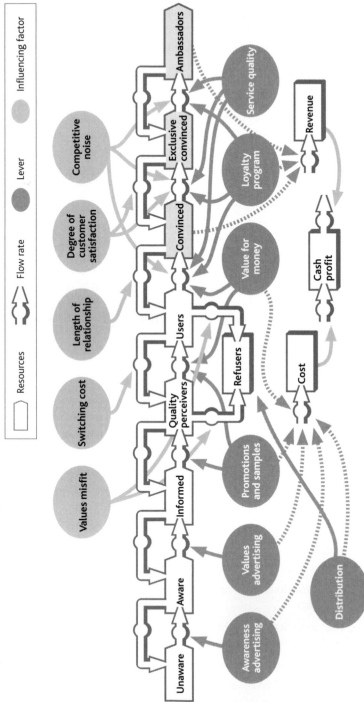

market and the choice chain. In the 1990s, the company's management developed a vision of establishing a leading role in the market by building on existing competencies and taking advantage of business opportunities arising from the advent of the Internet era. By mid-2000, Exodus had realized its ambition. Yet just a year later, it filed for bankruptcy. What had gone wrong?

In an emerging market, there are few customers using a service but a large pool of potential customers. Over time, as people sign up to one provider or another, the resource of potential customers depletes. At a certain stage, the net value of adding incremental new customers falls below the value of retaining existing customers. Exodus's management failed to recognize this crucial "inflection point" when its priority should have shifted from acquiring customers to retaining them. As a result, it continued to devote time and resources to growth initiatives when it should have been paying attention to stemming customer losses.

If we look at the choice chain diagram in Exhibit 4.9, we can see that different management levers and influencing factors affect the flows at different stages. The levers required to move people along the choice chain are not all related to marketing. Far from it: marketing is just one weapon in a company's armoury to promote customer choice. Other important levers can be applied to influence product quality, service, skills, staff numbers, and innovation.

For personal care company Gillette, a strategy of continuous innovation is central to earning customer choice. The company has recognized that if it fails to innovate, competitors will catch up and start to compete for its customers. To stay ahead of the game, it launches new products or variants at frequent intervals. These products are often based on advanced technologies that will take rival companies years to copy, thus affording Gillette a window of competitive advantage.

Careful analysis of the customer choice chain will reveal where the greatest opportunities lie for improving any flow rate and what the relevant actions are likely to cost. A detailed understanding of critical levers will allow management to assess whether the resources it is allocating to marketing and other areas are having the desired effect. It also enables a company to look beyond marketing and see whether *every* activity in its strategic and operational agenda is aligned with the need to compete for choice.

Exhibit 4.10 illustrates how the leverage in one company's choice chain varies at different stages and for different consumer segments. As we saw in the Exodus case, leverage also varies over time as stocks accumulate and deplete. Companies therefore need to conduct leverage analyses on a regular basis.

Exhibit 4.10
Quantifying leverage

Example: US consumer goods company
Incremental sales from a change of 2 percentage points in flow

Retention: Reducing out-flow by 2%	
Men 18–28	11.1%
Women 18–28	10.3%
Men 29–50	9.7%
Women 29–50	8.5%
Ageing 50+	6.3%

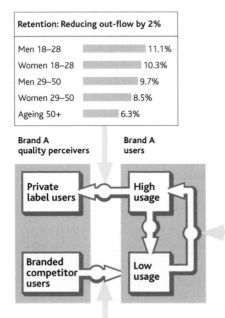

Brand A quality perceivers **Brand A users**

Private label users — High usage

Branded competitor users — Low usage

Share of requirement: Increasing usage among existing customers by 2%	
Men 18–28	8.5%
Ageing 50+	7.3%
Women 18–28	7.1%
Women 29–50	7.0%
Men 29–50	2.8%

Penetration: Increasing in-flow by 2%	
Women 29–50	8.3%
Men 29–50	6.5%
Men 18–28	4.9%
Women 18–28	4.3%
Ageing 50+	3.3%

Source: TNS 2002; Vanguard analysis

One further benefit of a clearly defined brand architecture is its suitability for scenario simulation modelling. It can easily be converted into a computerized resource model and then populated with data to create an immensely valuable tool. Managers can use it to test different strategies and analyze their outcomes over time in a risk-free environment. Such models work in a similar way to the flight simulators used in pilot training

Aligning values systems

Intimately linked to both a company's strategic principle and its ability to generate consumer choice is its values system. From a branding point of view, three values systems are central (Exhibit 4.11):

Corporate values. These constitute the identity of a business, and are often articulated in its strategic principle. They determine and constrain the way a company thinks about its proposition, its brand, and its market. Corporate values are those to which a company adheres in conducting its business and defining its role in society.

Brand values. A company will engineer a set of brand values (and thus the brand image) on the basis of its corporate values (identity). So, starting from a particular set of values one company may fashion one brand image while another company comes up with an altogether different image even though both brands are intended for the same customer segments. Companies seek to communicate their brand values in such a way as to maximize "values fit": a match with the values of target consumers that will earn their price acceptance and thus choice.

Consumer values. These are the guiding principles, beliefs, or mental models to which people adhere in interacting with others and leading their lives. An individual's values system influences his or her aspirations and actions; evolves slowly over time; and often varies by continent and country. Most of us live by a number of values that together make up our values system. Research shows that people tend to seek out others with similar values. Equally, they embrace concepts, ideas, or brands that closely match their own values.

If we look at the factors that drive consumer choice and the acceptance of a price premium, research shows that the values fit between brand and consumer is considerably more important than consumer purchasing power.[3] In other words, consumers are more willing to pay a price premium when there is a high degree of values fit.

This holds true for all consumers in all economic categories. Exhibit 4.12 shows that in the absence of values fit, few people – whether their purchasing power is high or low – are willing to pay a premium. However, people with low purchasing power are almost three times more willing to pay a premium if they perceive a high degree of values fit.

As society changes, so do consumer values. Companies that fail to monitor and respond to these changes can easily go off the rails and lose customers' continuing choice.

Exhibit 4.11
Core values systems

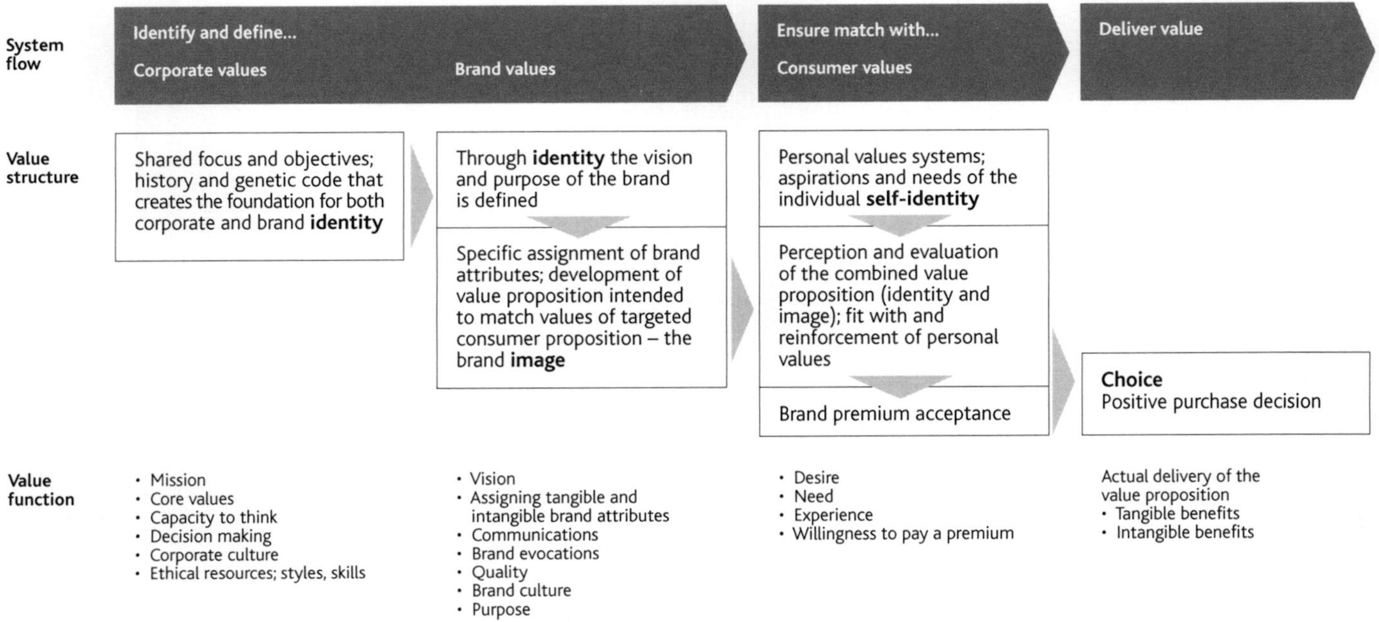

System flow	Identify and define... Corporate values	Brand values	Ensure match with... Consumer values	Deliver value

Value structure	Shared focus and objectives; history and genetic code that creates the foundation for both corporate and brand **identity**	Through **identity** the vision and purpose of the brand is defined	Personal values systems; aspirations and needs of the individual **self-identity**	
		Specific assignment of brand attributes; development of value proposition intended to match values of targeted consumer proposition – the brand **image**	Perception and evaluation of the combined value proposition (identity and image); fit with and reinforcement of personal values	**Choice** Positive purchase decision
			Brand premium acceptance	

| Value function | • Mission
 • Core values
 • Capacity to think
 • Decision making
 • Corporate culture
 • Ethical resources; styles; skills | • Vision
 • Assigning tangible and intangible brand attributes
 • Communications
 • Brand evocations
 • Quality
 • Brand culture
 • Purpose | • Desire
 • Need
 • Experience
 • Willingness to pay a premium | Actual delivery of the value proposition
 • Tangible benefits
 • Intangible benefits |

Exhibit 4.12
Values fit and the brand premium
Percentage of the population willing to pay a brand premium

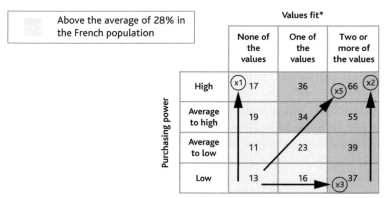

		Values fit*		
Above the average of 28% in the French population		None of the values	One of the values	Two or more of the values
High		(x1) 17	36	(x5) 66 (x2)
Average to high		19	34	55
Average to low		11	23	39
Low		13	16	(x3) 37

(Purchasing power — vertical axis label)

* In terms of five key values: ethical, mythical, emotional, self-identity, and economic.
Source: Megabrand, France, 1994

Consider UK mass-market retailer Marks & Spencer. Once a market leader with a solid reputation for quality and value, it lost sight of how its customers' needs and wants were changing. Although operating profits grew strongly from 1995 to 1998, its reputation for quality had started to decline as early as 1991. This change in perception should have been an important lead indicator for the company's management. Loyal customers finally lost patience with being short-changed, and revenues and profits tumbled in 1999, shocking investors, analysts, and journalists alike.

By January 2001, Marks & Spencer had earned the dubious distinction of becoming the company that had destroyed the most shareholder value in the previous three years; no other company in the FTSE 350 had subjected its investors to such a sharp fall in returns. It has taken two and a half years of hard work and renewed focus on the customer for M&S to begin to regain some of its former luster.

Or consider Levi Strauss's fortunes in the 1990s. Here was a brand that had carved out a global position for itself and was now exploiting advanced technology to offer customers jeans that were custom-fitted to their individual measurements. But as so often happens, the seeds of downfall were being sown even as the company's growth appeared unstoppable.

Sure enough, Levi's was innovating – but it wasn't the right sort of innovation. It was technology led, not market led. The company didn't try to match the renewal of its product lines to emerging fashion trends. The result: Levi's market share in men's jeans plummeted from a high of

48 percent in 1990 to 25 percent in 1998. It has since recouped much of this loss by rethinking its approach to innovation and customer segmentation and introducing new lines such as its Engineered jeans.

Understanding values is crucial to competing for choice. The fit or mismatch between the values projected by a brand and the values of individual stakeholders will determine whether the brand earns choice and justifies its price premium, or generates refusal.

Now let's consider an example of good values fit. Such is the enthusiasm for Harley-Davidson motorcycles that the Harley Owners' Club is the largest of its kind in the world, with some 660,000 members. The company has come a long way from the 1960s, when it almost ceased trading after the Japanese launched a new wave of cheaper, better-quality bikes in the US market. Harley-Davidson's resurgence has made it the strongest motorcycle brand in the country, and possibly the best-known in the world.

But the company is still facing a big challenge: how to attract younger consumers without alienating its main customer base – the baby-boomers who make up more than half of its market. A fifth are over 55; only about 17 percent are 35 or younger. To tackle the problem, the company has begun to introduce new models such as the V-Rod, its first completely new bike in 50 years, which is similar to the more technically oriented racing bikes made by such competitors as Honda and Yamaha.

Harley-Davidson has also set up a motorcycling safety course to target new consumers. As an executive said in an interview, "We obviously recognize that the baby-boomer generation is getting older, but we think there's still a long road to go with that group. We expect the V-Rod will bring in new, younger customers as well as appeal to our existing base."[4]

As with other resources in a choice chain, values accumulate or deplete over time, and need to be reinforced. With its new launch, Harley-Davidson is building relevant new values such as modernity and hedonism, while reinforcing existing values such as vitality and freedom. This case serves to illustrate how companies can track the different values of different age groups and respond with new products that allow younger generations to establish a values fit with their brands.

In the not too far distant future, performance comprehension will be informed by metrics that are not commonly discussed in management debates today. The main differences will be the monitoring of key resource flows and levels in a broader systemic context; a much higher level of detail; and the inclusion of many intangible components that are not currently measured. Taking steps to establish such comprehensive structures and capabilities sooner rather than later is likely to provide early movers with a competitive advantages. We go on to look at some of these steps in the final chapter.

Notes

1 Kevin Lane Keller, *Strategic Brand Management: Building, measuring, and managing brand equity* (Prentice-Hall, Upper Saddle River, NJ, 1998), p. 2.

2 Niall FitzGerald, "Life and death in the world of brands," *Market Leader*, Issue 14, Autumn 2001, p. 18.

3 Research conducted by Megabrand in France in 1994.

4 Nick Thornton, "Is the hog's future roadkill?," *www.brandchannel.com*, 10 September 2001.

5

Building brand competencies
for competitive advantage

Main themes

- The brand is probably the only entity in a business that can't be outsourced. Strategic branding is a core competency that must be cultivated to world-class standards *within* a company. It calls for leading-edge brand intelligence, systems, and structures and a team with cross-functional expertise and a focus on long-term value delivery.

- The CEO must be a passionate and proactive brand steward. With overall responsibility for business performance, overarching clarity on brand vision and values, and the ability to make cross-functional decisions, it is in fact the CEO who manages the brand.

- The CEO will also seek to establish the right mindset so that everyone in the organization, regardless of function, contributes to competing for choice every minute of every day and thus shares responsibility for brand management.

- In the future, companies will use strategy simulation tools to explore scenarios through modeling. Instead of conducting brand reviews, they will conduct brand previews. The implications in terms of decision-making skills, analytics, intelligence, and performance will be far-reaching.

Taking steps to build strategic branding competencies will confer competitive advantage on early movers.

Over the past decade, outsourcing has become increasingly important in a number of industries. There are often good reasons to outsource to external organizations that are specialists or that can provide services or products more effectively than you can. Many companies now outsource not just peripheral activities but core functions such as human resources, distribution, manufacturing, R&D, and customer services. Indeed, it appears that outsourcing has migrated up the corporate hierarchy to cover more and more critical functions (Exhibit 5.1).

Exhibit 5.1
Outsourcing spreads – but not branding

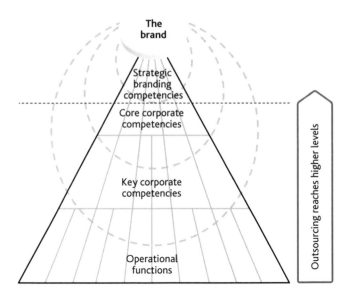

The management thinker Tom Peters has argued that a company can outsource everything, including the chief executive. Whatever the merits of that argument, we believe that a brand can't be outsourced. It embodies a company's identity and values. In addition, it serves as a basis for establishing clear objectives for value delivery that can be shared throughout the organization and with external partners and suppliers. Clearly, this isn't something to delegate to third-party providers.

When a company *does* outsource functions or processes, it must make sure there are well-defined standards and principles relating to quality, delivery, ethics, and so on to which all parties adhere. Again, the brand acts as the focal point here, linking customers, company, and suppliers of outsourced functions and helping in the management of these relationships and in the maintenance of quality delivery standards. Indeed, a clearly articulated brand architecture can make collaborations with third parties much more effective, since it gives the company intelligence and insights that enable it to provide a tightly focused brief and allows the external agency to concentrate on finding creative solutions to meet these specific objectives.

Some companies have gone a long way toward articulating their strategic principle and embedding it in the organization with the brand as the focal point. The brand then comes to embody the company's promise to its various stakeholders, and its ethics in conducting its business. Dell, for example, states that "the company's direct model starts and ends with our customers. With the power of direct and our team of talented people, we are able to provide customers with superb value, high-quality, relevant technology, customized systems, superior services and support, and products and services that are easy to buy."

Just as the brand can't be outsourced, neither can strategic brand management competencies. They are central to understanding how to compete and for what choice – and to ensuring this is done effectively. Building strategic branding competencies should thus be a priority for every company.

The role of the CEO

The approach we have outlined in this book takes us well beyond the idea that the brand manager should be the steward of the brand. On the contrary, this role belongs to the chief executive, who is ultimately responsible for:

- Articulating the strategic principle: the company's mission, vision, and values.

- Establishing a view of the complete resource system and how it can be leveraged to compete for choice – or in other words, bringing the consumer into the boardroom.

- Aligning everyone throughout the organization to compete for choice continuously and effectively.

- Building and championing the resource system for the long term.

Why should it be the CEO who is ultimately responsible for brand management, and not the marketing manager, the vice-president of branding, or even the HR manager? In a classic organizational structure, the only area where there is a dedicated manager responsible for an entire stakeholder choice chain is human resources. It is unlikely there will be a customer resources manager or partner resources manager to oversee their respective choice chains. Instead, managers are usually assigned to functions such as marketing, sales, manufacturing, and logistics. This means that the various levers within an individual choice chain are under the control of different people, making it difficult to achieve a coherent bird's-eye view on how effectively the choice chain is managed.

It is the CEO's job to ensure that all stakeholders are managed in a way that drives the business forward. This involves taking responsibility for strategic direction; assigning ownership for each stakeholder choice chain; ensuring activities are properly coordinated across the organization; and realigning research and intelligence to provide necessary data on resource levels and flow rates. To perform these functions effectively, the CEO will need to adopt a holistic view of the brand as a system of resources – a view that recognizes the interconnections and reinforcing effects between the different stakeholder chains.

Much current management literature views the CEO's primary role as creating value for shareholders. Though the idea sounds fine in principle, the focus on creating wealth for investors is too narrow, and disregards the company's obligation to deliver value to other stakeholders such as employees and customers. The recent telecoms bust, in which operators persuaded investors to give them capital to build capacity but didn't manage to attract enough customers to pay for the services they offered, illustrates what can happen when a company's stakeholder focus is misaligned and symmetry of choice is not achieved.

Some CEOs may be reluctant to take charge of brand management because they think it is too "operational." Not so. As we have seen, brand management is about much more than marketing: it touches every function within a company and involves high-level management decisions that go way beyond the control of individual functional managers. Only the CEO has a truly global perspective on the enterprise, its environment, and its evolution through time; only the CEO is in a position to make dispassionate decisions about resource allocation across the various functions in the best interests of the organization as a whole.

There are no two ways about it: the ultimate brand custodian can only be the CEO. As well as deciding which choices to compete for and how, the CEO must establish a "brand-committed" organization where the whole company, from the line worker to the receptionist to the sales representative, shares the goal of continuously competing for choice. That means every individual is aware how his or her actions can shape stakeholders' perceptions of the brand and thereby contribute to the success of the enterprise.

The CEO must also manage and develop the *raison d'être* of the brand, and ensure its longevity by passing on a healthy brand resource system to his or her successor.

Since the brand is the focal point for all stakeholders, how could brand management *not* be the CEO's domain? In some leading luxury and consumer goods companies, chief executives have already made brand management an explicit strategic priority. Their example will doubtless be followed by many others in the executive suites of the future as businesses come to understand the importance of competing for choice.

Team power

Central though the CEO is to brand management, the necessary strategic competencies can't be confined to a single pair of hands but must be dispersed throughout and embedded in the whole organization. Although it is the CEO who is ultimately responsible for performance, part of the job of being a good brand steward is to establish a high-performing team with cross-functional experience to develop brand strategy. Two things make such a team essential.

First, effective performance comprehension and management calls for a full and detailed picture of the business and its objectives. Only a cross-functional team led by the CEO can hope to develop a truly holistic understanding of the workings of the company as a system. Few third-party service providers – advertisers, market research agencies, management consultants – are capable of achieving this kind of understanding, so it is difficult for them to make truly informed and objective recommendations. Without a holistic perspective, there is always a risk that a course of action that feels right for one part of the business will have unforeseen and possibly damaging knock-on effects in another.

Second, a high-performing cross-functional team with a solid grasp of the brand architecture represents a reservoir of experience, knowledge, and skills that can help a company stay on track if it should lose its CEO or other key executives. Top talent is highly mobile and in short supply. Even if the company manages to recruit an impressive replacement from elsewhere, the skills a new CEO brings may prove less potent in a new setting: consider Doug Ivester at Coca-Cola, or the superstars from GE who seem unable to replicate their success outside its well-oiled machine. Together, the brand architecture and team structure provide a mechanism for capturing and accumulating implicit knowledge and dispersing it throughout the organization, so making the company less vulnerable to changes in the executive suite and helping newcomers quickly get up to speed on the way the business works.

Key brand capabilities

We have identified five main areas in which CEOs should seek to establish solid capabilities to support strategic and tactical initiatives for their brands:

- **Brand visioning.** This involves decoding qualitative and quantitative intelligence on internal capabilities; surveying the consumer, market, and competitive environment to articulate a compelling strategic principle for the organization to act upon; and setting the agenda for innovation and renewal.

- **Brand charting.** This is about mapping the full set of brand resources market by market to establish an accurate visual picture of the workings of the brand that management can use as a common point of reference in debating initiatives, and monitoring structural changes and updating the architecture as necessary.

- **Brand analytics.** This entails populating the brand architecture with detailed time-based intelligence on levels, flows, and values of tangible and intangible resources; identifying sources of growth (from where will how many new customers emerge?); quantifying leverage points in the system by segment; monitoring lead performance indicators; decoding performance results; and triggering research to explore the underlying factors influencing performance.

- **Brand modelling.** This consists of establishing plausible market and brand scenarios; recognizing the principles of flows, stock accumulation, and non-linear interdependencies; undertaking dynamic modelling to quantify the impact of different initiatives and identify any synergies between them; and analyzing the outcomes of the modelling exercise to select the best possible strategy and most effective sequencing of initiatives.

- **Brand execution.** This means establishing excellence in the process of delivering value to all stakeholders; aligning execution with the image and spirit of the brand so that retail and service standards reflect the values of the core consumer segment; ensuring that product or service delivery happens at the right time and place and to the right quality; and organizing execution by choice chain in order to leverage capabilities fully and secure long-term value creation.

Exhibit 5.2
Aspirations for brand management

	Poor brand practice (Past)	Standard brand practice (Present)	Best brand practice (Future)
Strategy	Formulated intuitively	Fact-based but static, with predominantly short-term profit focus	Fact-based and dynamically informed, with focus on long-term value delivery to stakeholders
Systems	No structured brand management system; very basic market research	Simple management elements Fragmented brand-oriented market research measuring past performance	Integrated system for dynamic brand value management, fed by comprehensive intelligence with hard and soft performance indicators (e.g. sales, morale, image perceptions)
Skills	Branding handled by sales and marketing	Business graduates enter as brand managers; emphasis on short-term profit performance	Executives and experienced managers have brand expertise and focus on value creation; continuous learning
Structure	Little integration Product managers	Branding is one of several functions; brand managers oversee separate hierarchies	Cross-functional brand management team; interaction between functions coordinated by a central group
Style	Top-down brand management; leadership without consensus "The brand is just the brand"; operational issues take priority	Brand management is a complex "black box" "We define our brand and its proposition for consumers"	Managing the brand as a resource system, recognizing that all entities influence its performance Clear stakeholder focus, with customer-driven development of distinctive value propositions Clear sense of what the brand stands for and where it is going

Exhibit 5.3
Building competitive advantage through a structured management process

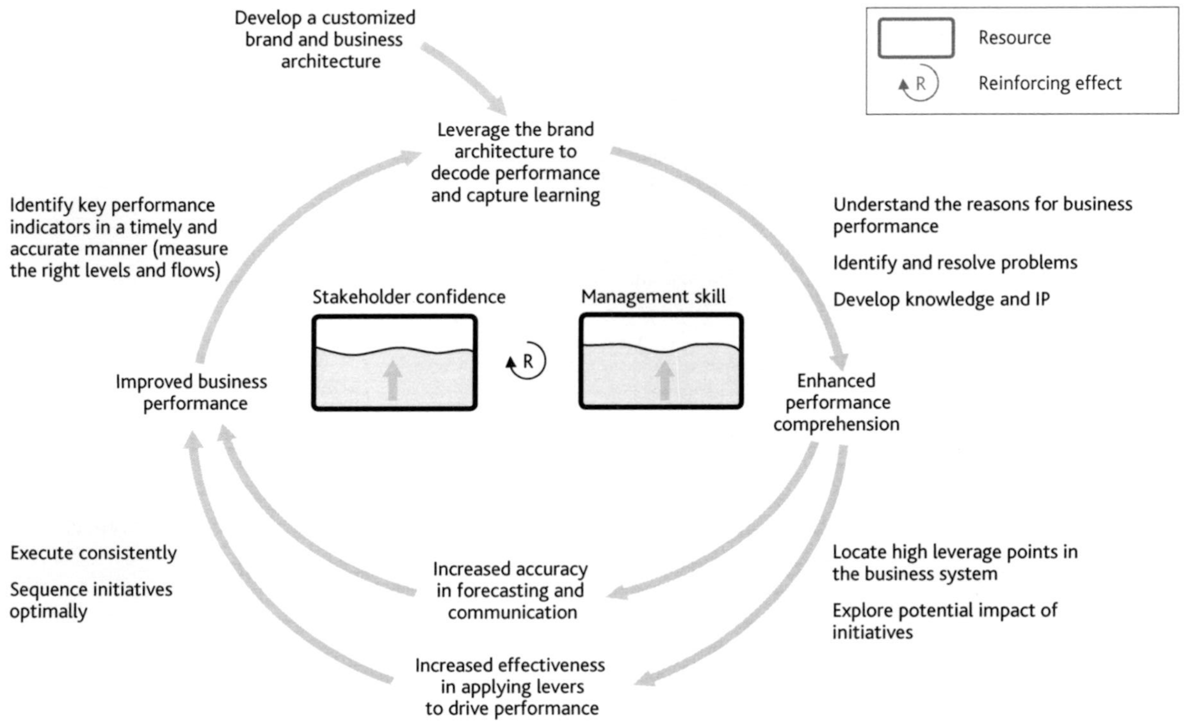

Develop a customized brand and business architecture

Leverage the brand architecture to decode performance and capture learning

Understand the reasons for business performance

Identify and resolve problems

Develop knowledge and IP

Enhanced performance comprehension

Locate high leverage points in the business system

Explore potential impact of initiatives

Management skill

Stakeholder confidence

R

Increased accuracy in forecasting and communication

Increased effectiveness in applying levers to drive performance

Improved business performance

Identify key performance indicators in a timely and accurate manner (measure the right levels and flows)

Execute consistently

Sequence initiatives optimally

Resource

Reinforcing effect

R

Taken together, these capabilities form the basis for developing robust brand strategies and marketing plans. Establishing and leveraging them isn't a one-off exercise; rather, it's a dynamic and self-reinforcing process, as illustrated in Exhibit 5.2.

The exhibit shows how a management team establishes performance comprehension, starts to apply initiatives more effectively, improves performance, and further enhances comprehension. The dynamics build over time as the team goes though successive iterations of the process. A few iterations will do far more to build management performance comprehension than any external party could achieve. The real competitive advantage comes as investors and other stakeholders grow more confident in management's grasp of the health of the business, and as levers are applied increasingly effectively to influence the system in the short and the long term.

Don't copy best practice – establish your own

Achieving best practice in branding should be at the top of any company's wish list; after all, this is what will determine its success at competing for choice. But as we saw in chapter 4, best practice is not something that can be imported from outside. Each organization needs to tailor the right combination of systems, skills, structure, and style for its own needs. Best practice can't be bought off the peg or borrowed from a "how to" strategy manual, but must be built from scratch around a company's unique resource system.

Exhibit 5.3 shows in simplified form the stages of evolution an organization might go through in order to establish its own best practice brand management. For many companies, the process begins with a charismatic leader – Phil Knight of Nike, say, or Jeff Bezos of Amazon – who has instinctively understood the concept of the brand resource system. But even the pioneers who create powerful new brands usually end up having to put in place structures and systems so as to sustain growth while staying true to the original brand concept.

And what of the CEO? In best practice brand management, the CEO will manage the business with a different mindset, with different intelligence, and with a different decision-making processes (Exhibit 5.4).

Exhibit 5.4
Implications of best practice brand management

	Classic brand management	Best practice brand management
Different mindset	The brand as a single asset	The brand as a constantly evolving resource system
	Short-term financial rigor in conflict with long-term marketing thinking	Shared focus on long-term sustainable value creation
	Brand management as a function (according to a manual)	Brand management as an organization-wide responsibility (according to a shared values system)
Different information	Mainly financial performance measurements (e.g. sales)	Broad range of integrative performance indicators (e.g. sales, loyalty, morale, service, conviction)
	Assumptions about "soft" intangible factors	Quantification of intangible factors
	Focus on "snapshot" values	Focus on rates of change (in-flows and out-flows)
Different decision-making processes	Standard solutions (e.g. one strategy applied throughout a national market)	Tailored solutions (e.g. regional and sub-markets, segment-based strategies)
	Debating what we should do	Debating the assumptions behind proposed courses of action
	Extrapolating from the past to predict the future (brand reviews)	Simulating the future (proactive brand previews)

Looking to the future

In chapter 4, we touched on the use of simulation modeling as an aid to strategic decision making. Just as pilots are trained on flight simulators that provide a safe environment in which to learn procedures, respond to unexpected events, and analyze the effects of their actions, so the companies of the future will use computerized scenario simulation tools to test and evaluate possible strategies in a risk-free setting. The effect on brand management will be profound.

No longer will managers have to rely on past history as a basis for forecasting future performance. Instead, they will be able to *explore* the future by modelling the various outcomes of possible initiatives. They will be able to see whether a promising strategy is likely to fail or, worse, backfire; select the best initiatives from a range of options, and sequence them in the most effective fashion; understand how an action in one part of the organization can have unexpected repercussions elsewhere; and determine where resources should best be dedicated to benefit the business as a whole. Indeed, so powerful are these tools that it is unlikely that stakeholders will be prepared to allow executives to manage the businesses of the future without them.

However, it would be a mistake to imagine that these tools will become a substitute for management experience, judgment, and intuition. Even though brand strategy will undoubtedly become far more analytical and fact based than it is today, creative skills will continue to be important. Analysis and creativity must go hand in hand, mutually reinforcing one another rather than fighting for turf.

Getting brand strategy right is no easy task. But applying the approach we have outlined in this book will start you off on the right track.

One of the essential steps is to develop and apply a series of complementary strategic branding capabilities. Another is to recognize the central role of the CEO in brand management. Yet another is to work out what best practice means for you rather than trying to emulate your competitors.

The questions companies usually ask themselves about branding are really about marketing: But they miss the point. As we have seen, far from being an isolated asset, the brand is inseparable from the business and the resource system that underpins it. To have any real meaning, questions about branding must be questions about strategy.

With this in mind, we end by posing a series of questions that will help your company to understand how effectively it competes for choice. Any leading brand-owning organization should be able to answer them with facts.

1 Do you ask people in your organization, "What are we competing for?" Would everyone come up with the same answer? Would it be the *right* answer?

2 Do you have a clear idea of where your future growth will come from? How much will be organic market growth, and how much will be share captured from your competitors? What is your strategy for winning over users of each individual rival brand?

3 Do you know where and how great your brand leverage is by segment? Is it in penetration (attracting new customers), share of requirement (increasing usage by existing customers), or retention (keeping users in the franchise)?

4 Do you have a clearly articulated and quantified choice chain for each of your key stakeholders? Does everyone in your organization know who is responsible for achieving what levels of choice by each of the stakeholders?

5 Do you know how much you need to spend, and on what levers, to maintain your current level of performance? And how much to spend to grow your brand in accordance with your plans for next year?

6 Do you have a robust brand architecture populated with fact-based intelligence to help you understand which management levers influence which choice drivers, and to what extent?

If you answer "No" to any of these questions, ask yourself one last question:

What is stopping me taking steps to address these issues?

Appendix: The evolution of business strategy

Strategy is about competing successfully. More specifically, it is about finding a way to beat present and potential competitors through superior execution while making a profit at the same time.

The theory of business strategy has undergone profound change in the past fifty years. Exhibit A shows how different fields within strategic theory have converged to produce today's sophisticated approaches.

The influence of Porter

The work done by Michael Porter in the 1980s, notably in his book *Competitive Strategy*,[1] stands as a milestone in the development of business strategy. It marks a shift away from corporate planning toward strategy formulation. Porter introduced the concept of generic strategies to represent the different options that can be pursued by players in a particular industry. In simple terms, these are cost leadership and the pursuit of differentiation. Which option a particular player chooses to pursue will depend on its circumstances and position in the market.

Porter also explored the role that organizational capabilities – defined as the capacity for undertaking a particular productive activity – play in a company's success, and introduced the value chain framework to help managers understand the structure and determinants of these capabilities.

Over time, as this approach was refined, the concept of sustainable strategy came to include position (choosing to perform activities in a different way from rivals), tradeoffs (the need to decide to do some things, but not others), and control (locking out imitators by creating a value delivery chain that is unique and hard to copy).

The resource-based view

In the late 1980s and early 1990s, strategy researchers turned their attention from a company's competitive environment and positioning to its internal resources and capabilities.[2] This shift was due in part to the increasing instability of the macroeconomic environment, which often invalidated strategies based on external factors, and in part to the realization that

Exhibit A
A concise overview of developments in business strategy
Key events and publications

Source: Edith T. Penrose, *The Theory of the Growth of the Firm* (Oxford University Press, 1959); Jay W. Forrester, *Industrial Dynamics* (MIT Press, 1961); Donella H. Meadows, *The Limits to Growth* (Universe Books, 1972); Russell L. Ackoff, *Redesigning the Future* (John Wiley, 1974); Michael E. Porter, *Competitive Strategy* (Free Press, 1980); Birger Wernerfelt, "A resource-based view of the firm," (*Strategic Management Journal*, 1984); Peter M. Senge, *The Fifth Discipline* (Currency Doubleday, 1990); Peter Schwartz, *The Art of the Long View* (Currency Doubleday, 1991); Donella H. Meadows, *Beyond the Limits* (Chelsea Green Publishing, 1992); Robert S. Kaplan and David P. Norton, *The Balanced Scorecard* (Harvard Business School Press, 1996); John D. Sterman, Business Dynamics (McGraw-Hill, 2000); Kim Warren, *Competitive Strategy Dynamics* (John Wiley, 2002).

profitability seems to be linked to differences between firms, rather than between the industries in which they compete.[3]

The resource-based view emphasizes the importance of managing a company's resources as elements in a system of stakeholders, and taking into account the interactions between these resources during performance evaluation.

Adding the dynamic perspective

More recent developments in strategy research combine the resource-based view and its concept of stock accumulation[4] with leading-edge strategic modeling tools and concepts.[5] They recognize that resources are not just a way of explaining past and present performance; they also play an important part in sustaining performance over time. As a result, a company's ability to leverage and grow its resources is inherently dynamic.

Competitive strategy dynamics

The starting point for this discipline is the challenge any leadership team faces: building performance through time. Since performance is determined more by management controls than by external conditions, management matters. It is the resources that have been built up and sustained through an organization's history that drive its performance today. The key to competitive advantage thus becomes a company's ability to accumulate and combine resources more effectively or faster than its rivals.[6]

Resources – customers, dealers, products, staff, cash, capacity, and so on – are finite and measurable, so strategy must be built on solid facts, not elusive concepts. Competitive strategy dynamics uses simple frameworks to capture the way in which resources accumulate and decay over time, the way they interact, and their impact on performance.

The strategic architecture produced by these efforts explains why an organization is performing as it does, thus eliminating much of the dispute that so often gets in the way of strategic decision making. The architecture also clarifies who needs to do what and when to improve performance, and makes it easy to communicate the findings to staff, business partners, investors, and any other groups who need to understand and participate in business development. Finally, it allows strategy and performance to be constantly updated to take account of changes in the organization and its environment.

Strategy has evolved from early static approaches focusing on competitive advantage to much more dynamic approaches that recognize the interdependencies both within any business resource system and between a company and its external environment. Customers and other stakeholders now occupy a much more prominent place in strategy formulation. At last, the consumer has made it into the boardroom.

Notes

1 Free Press, New York, 1980.

2 Birger Wernerfelt, "A resource-based view of the firm," *Strategic Management Journal*, 1984, Volume 5, Issue 2, pp. 171–80.

3 Empirical research demonstrates that differences between companies account for more than twice the variation in profits as differences in industry conditions. *See* Anita M. McGahan and Michael E. Porter, "How much does industry matter, really?," *Strategic Management Journal*, 1997, Volume 18, Issue S1, pp. 15–30.

4 Ingemar Dierickx and Karel Cool, "Asset stock accumulation and sustainability of competitive advantage," *Management Science*, 1989, Volume 35, Number 12, pp. 1504–11.

5 John D. Sterman, *Business Dynamics: Systems thinking and modeling for a complex world* (McGraw-Hill, New York, 2000).

6 Kim Warren, *Competitive Strategy Dynamics* (John Wiley, New York, 2002).

Also by Vola Press

The Critical Path

The fundamental challenge facing business leaders is to drive performance into the future. To tackle it effectively, they need a clear understanding of what causes performance to improve or deteriorate over time and what power they have to change this trajectory for the better. Without such an understanding, they risk making poor choices about their future, either by failing to exploit promising opportunities or else by pursuing objectives they can never achieve.

The Critical Path sets the agenda for building business strategy. It seeks to provide managers with sound answers to three crucial questions:

- Why is our business performance following its current path?

- Where is it going if we carry on as we are?

- How can we design a robust strategy to transform this performance in the future?

Existing management tools and approaches offer little help with these issues. Here, we provide reliable, practical frameworks that combine to create a living picture of how an enterprise actually works. They show you how to find the levers that are under your control, and how to choose the right ones to accomplish your specific goals. They suggest how you can defeat competitors in your efforts to develop your future, and deal with the powerful external forces that can thwart your plans or work in your favor.

The Critical Path is the road your organization travels in order to build and sustain the resources and capabilities that will shape its future. This book provides a practical, in-depth guide to help you in this difficult but rewarding journey.

The Critical Path
Building strategic performance through time
Kim Warren

UK £15.00 · US $24.00

Also by Vola Press

People Power

People are an expensive, critical resource in any organization, and can represent a powerful source of sustained advantage. They profoundly affect other resources, such as customers, brand reputation, intellectual property, and cash. They drive the growth or decline of these resources and possess attributes of their own, such as skills and knowledge, that must be carefully developed and nurtured.

Despite this, leaders tend to focus on the softer aspects of people management – those that are the least easy to identify and influence, such as motivating, mentoring, and teamworking – while neglecting the fundamentals of how many people they need, where, when, and to do what. This book redresses the balance, providing a practical, rigorous, and fact-based approach to managing this most sensitive of resources.

People Power:

- Shows leaders how to understand and manage the changes in their staff base over time in the light of often complex interactions between hiring, promotion, development, and attrition.

- Explains where people connect to the tangible resources of the business to help managers deploy them more effectively, get the right number of the best people in the right places, and make the necessary adjustments as the business changes through time.

- Describes the mechanisms by which people and teams develop skills and shared capabilities so that they can boost the performance of the organization as a whole.

- Provides a common language in diagrams, words, and numbers to help leaders, HR professionals, and others in the management team understand and communicate how their staff resources are developing through time, thus enabling costly and arduous organizational initiatives to be undertaken with confidence and support.

Improving performance by making better decisions about your people is not just a matter for top management; given the right tools, anyone with influence over the way their enterprise works can make a difference. This book provides an original approach to developing organizational effectiveness that is long overdue.

People Power
Developing the talent to perform
Kim Warren & Jeremy Kourdi
UK £15.00 · US $24.00

 **strategy**dynamics

Visit *www.strategydynamics.com*

Strategy Dynamics enables you to build an integrated and fact-based picture of how the resources of your business are developing through time, as a result of their mutual interdependence, management policies and external opportunities and constraints.

The global resource for information about the Strategy Dynamics approach is *www.strategydynamics.com*. On the site you will find a wealth of information including:

- **Simulation software**
- **Publications**
- **Learning materials**
- **Training solutions**
- **Management development**
- **Executive coaching**

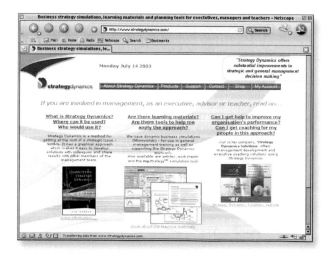